Tall
Poppy

Tall Poppy

How to Lead without Losing Your Head

Holly McKissick

Abingdon Press
Nashville

TALL POPPY
HOW TO LEAD WITHOUT LOSING YOUR HEAD

Copyright © 2013 by Abingdon Press

All rights reserved.
No part of this work may be reproduced or transmitted in any form or by any means, electronic or mechanical, including photocopying and recording, or by any information storage or retrieval system, except as may be expressly permitted by the 1976 Copyright Act or in writing from the publisher. Requests for permission should be addressed to Permissions, The United Methodist Publishing House, P.O. Box 801, 201 Eighth Avenue South, Nashville, TN 37202-0801 or permissions@umpublishing.org.

This book is printed on acid-free paper.

Library of Congress Cataloging-in-Publication Data

McKissick, Holly.
  Tall poppy : how to lead without losing your head / Holly McKissick.
    pages cm
  ISBN 978-1-4267-5284-1 (pbk. : alk. paper) 1. Leadership—Religious aspects—Christianity. 2. Risk taking (Psychology)—Religious aspects—Christianity. I. Title.
  BV4597.53.L43M46 2013
  253—dc23

2013011503

All scripture quotations unless noted otherwise are taken from the *New Revised Standard Version of the Bible,* copyright 1989, Division of Christian Education of the National Council of the Churches of Christ in the United States of America. Used by permission. All rights reserved.

13 14 15 16 17 18 19 20 21 22 —10 9 8 7 6 5 4 3 2 1
MANUFACTURED IN THE UNITED STATES OF AMERICA

CONTENTS

Introduction vii

Chapter One
Leaders Put Their Spades in First 1

Chapter Two
Leaders Build 27

Chapter Three
Leaders Find Water Even in the Desert 49

Chapter Four
Leaders Part the Waters of Conflict and Discontent 75

Chapter Five
Leaders Weed and Prune 101

Chapter Six
Leaders Catch the Wind of the Spirit 119

INTRODUCTION

It has to be the worst advice I've ever received: "Start a new church, but lay low." I heard it from more than one person in a key leadership position after the soul-wrenching end to a twenty-one-year ministry at the church I served as the founding pastor.

I tried to imagine Jesus saying that. Lay low. Don't do anything that could attract criticism or attention. We want your energy, passion, creativity; but we don't want the risks associated with those leadership traits. Give it a few months until things have died down. Thank God I had two teenagers whom I needed to provide for. Even if I hadn't needed the work, I could hear the word from Ecclesiastes: *carpe diem*. Seize the day. That's all you have.

What I had was eighteen months before my daughter would graduate from high school, eighteen months to get my family resettled, to get something up and running. I thought of the grocery list she left on the refrigerator after the only church she had ever known had imploded, taking with it our spiritual, emotional, and financial ground.

needs:

peppers

hummus

shampoo

conditioner

New family

New religion

Not a bad list.

When the Buddhist center surfaced as a possible home for our new church, I thought of her list. Not a new religion, but at least a new start, a fresh home, an open space.

As is often the case, her gut was right.

The decision to plant a church in a Buddhist temple, to build our nest in an interfaith tree, was gracious and healing, replenishing and hopeful, particularly for me. Who would have guessed that a pastor would find herself taken in, given a place in the inn, by the Buddhists? I shouldn't have been surprised. The mission of the center is *to be the most spiritually welcoming home in the community.*

Along with healing, the decision felt creative, novel, strategic even. Few Christians in our community worshiped in an interfaith home. We would be among the first to move from the familiar space of control and dominance to the unfamiliar land of surrender and dependence. There could be some rewards to planting in the Rime Buddhist Center, putting our spade in first. The choice communicated who we were—theologically and socially—to the neighborhood and community: an open-minded, progressive faith community.

There was more to it, though. The experience of being cut down, after leaving my former church, was by far the most searing experience of my life, leaving a deep gash in my spirit. I needed to be welcomed, accepted, and received—that was the list on *my* refrigerator. And that's what I found when I took my shoes off and walked on new holy ground.

So, I was surprised and saddened when a group of colleagues expressed their dismay about the Buddhist center: *I could never get my church to agree to that.* Yet, the cautious, reserved, risk-averse approach that shaped their ministry was understandable. Many had adopted and honed that pattern after experiences of being swiped at, cut down.

In New Zealand, they have a name for such behavior; they refer to it as the "Tall Poppy Syndrome." Many in that culture maintain a low profile, as they know that those who stand tall are liable to get their blossoms or their heads cut off. But, as leaders know, although tall poppies may be vulnerable, they also have the best view of the landscape and horizon.

The truth is that we pastors follow One whose organic, visionary, authentic, vulnerable leadership cost him his life. What should we expect as pastors who are called to follow his witness, challenging the religious and political systems that marginalize and exclude? Should we expect betrayal, attack, and even crucifixion? There is no avoiding that part of the story for any leader who pushes the boundaries. But the Christian story ends not on a cross but in a community created to bring God's healing, peace, justice. I'm writing this book to share what I've learned from standing tall for twenty-five years, twenty-one of which were spent in the church I founded. My story, my song if you will, is composed of four births—a girl, a boy, and two congregations. Tall Poppy style of leading is, most days, enlivening and empowering; and it influences growth and maturity, contingent upon my role as leader.

This book is meant to help you discover and reap the benefits of Tall Poppy leadership. It is meant to help you stand tall even in the face of failure and the hurtful actions of others. But it's also meant to help you keep your eye on the prize, on the faithfulness of the One who, as the twenty-third Psalm tells us, walks before us, beside us, and behind us, providing us with the instruments, instruction, and inspiration to create our own song.

When I was writing this book, my daughter was taking high school biology. The dining table was a jumbled mess of paper. Sorting through the piles, she said, "cytoskeleton . . . that is what you are writing about, that is what makes it possible for the tall poppy to stand." She was right; plants could not stand or defy gravity without a cytoskeleton. Plants rely on the cytoskeleton to exhibit *gravitropism*—the ability to stand tall, to face upward, despite the immeasurable atmospheric pressure pushing down on them. A Tall Poppy remains inherently vulnerable, however, to being cut down. But do not let this discourage you from blossoming. *I* have been cut down; my roots have been stripped from the earth. Still I held together, and my faith in Tall Poppy leadership remains. Of significant value is what I have learned because of the loss of a dream and community that I birthed and nurtured. Like anyone in a similar situation, I experienced loss and personal grief, which is, to some extent, inexplicable and inexpressible.

But bad things are survivable, and they don't prevent God from giving us good gifts in the future. Every Sunday, we open our worship at Peace Church with a refrain I learned from a Tall Poppy preacher who got cut and stood tall: God is good, all the time, and all the time, God is good. God will have the final say; this sustains my resilience; this is my gravitropism. After the first cut, when I was too numb even to hear the music, my mentors provided me with a lyric I can now sing: *this is the best thing that ever happened to you.* They couldn't have been more right. I have come to know, as a dear friend and colleague says, "Where you land, there's your gold."

Come; let us be Tall Poppies together. I hope for you a song in the wind.

Thanks be to God.

chapter one

Leaders Put Their Spades in First

Building a church or a new ministry program or anything, for that matter, from scratch, takes more than nerve; it takes courage. It takes leadership, vision, and listening for God's prompting. To get to the harvest, it first takes a leader to begin the spadework with intentional planning and excitement for new possibilities. This chapter explores the benefits and risks of Tall Poppy leadership. Tall Poppy leaders attract attention—leaving a mark on the landscape, shaping the environment, and preparing the soil for others. Such leaders have a clear view to get the lay of the land. They reap the benefits of being the first to harvest, but they are easy targets to be picked or cut down.

> **Tall Poppy leaders have the best view but can be easy targets.**

Tall Poppy Leaders Create a New Future

When a revolutionary architecture team from the Bay Area came to Kansas with unorthodox building methods, they created a brilliant, unique church campus and inspired innovative, sustainable practices in the Midwest. That church was Saint Andrew in Olathe, Kansas, my first church plant. But the initial decision to use this firm came from a leader's vision. Such leadership entails risks. Tallness attracts the attention of smallness and small-mindedness; disease and dysfunction are threatened by health and productivity. Along with imitation and flattery, Tall Poppies attract envy and even annihilation. Kris Culp's work *Vulnerability and Glory: A Theological Account* (Louisville: Westminster John Knox Press, 2010) offers both an astute theological reading of this tension and the painful experiences of many gifted church pastors.

Without minimizing the cost or challenge, Tall Poppy leaders embrace the possibility of leadership. They strive toward creating a new heaven and a new earth. South African writer Antjie Kroc writes powerfully about the much-longed-for transformation in her country. Keenly aware of the dominance and privilege afforded to her as a white South African, Kroc used her pen as a tool to unearth the injustice embedded in her country and to plant seedlings for new land. Kroc epitomizes the capacity of a Tall Poppy leader: laying the very foundations of the new place we are headed. This is the opportunity that pastors need to take hold of. Why? Because we follow a risen Savior—One who leads us to live as he did, forgiving every misstep and wrong turn. Jesus of Nazareth, who saw his own ability to lead, rose up like a Tall Poppy, taking the risks that his followers are called to take.

"It's Never Been Done Before"

If I heard him say it once, I heard Gary Black say it a thousand times during the ten-year span of our building project. Gary, a professor of engineering and architecture, and his way of living in the world are innovative, mold-making, and mold-breaking. A natural teacher, Gary transformed every conversation during our project into an exchange of ideas, a laboratory for never-before-attempted solutions. He'd run his lanky fingers through his hair and then pull out a pen and napkin and start sketching, like the straw-bale church he designed for our faith community on the Kansas prairie: "First you build a rebar structure, and then you stack bales of hay and shoot it with shotcrete. The walls have the rich, warm feel of adobe, with a fraction of the cost. You get a gorgeous, sustainably built building, eco-friendly and energy efficient, with the materials you make sewers from. This church will be the first of its kind in the Midwest."

People thought Gary and his younger partners, Cullen Burda and Kyriakos Pontikis, were crazy—way too "out there." It didn't help that they came from Berkeley, California, as far as you can get, figuratively, from Olathe, Kansas. Stepping off the plane with survey stakes and orange flags, they looked like magi from the Far East, or west.

When they camped on the church property during the design phase in order to better observe all the ways in which light interacted with the land, we knew our church home would be a unique expression of our faith, environment, and values. And we were right; the result was awe-inspiring in both design and structure and was designed to be efficient and inexpensive. However, the creation came at a considerable cost: significant stress and tension over a decade-long building phase.

Hiring architects from the Bay Area raised more than eyebrows; it raised anxiety levels, too. As I look back at an over-twenty-years-ago Holly, I recognize that I was slow to respond to divergent views and opinions. At times, I failed to hear the concerns and heed the objections of members, in part, because such responses went hand in hand with strong emotions. Just because I was the designated leader didn't mean that I was perfect or even made the best decisions all the time. On the contrary, I learned a lot.

In the face of the concrete challenge, I put my head down and pushed harder. Of course, I wanted to be liked, and I wanted to get along. And, honestly, I wanted folks to go along with my ideas, which I believed in, strongly. I could see the emotional and financial cost of the project, but I minimized the toll that such an innovative project would extract from the congregation. My heart was focused on the possibility of creation. It was one of a kind. It had never been done. It was wondrous and winsome.

Tall Poppy Leaders Have a Different View

Here's the challenge that many Tall Poppy leaders face: we have a different view of the world. We see things, not as they are, but as they can be. We want to be the change we wish to see in the world. We lead from a place of authenticity and heart. And we grow taller as we profit from our missteps. But to reap the benefits we need to develop a proactive stance, anticipating uncomfortable reactions and attending, adequately and thoughtfully, to questions and concerns.

> **Tall Poppy leaders see things as they can be.**

"Hmmm . . . and how many *churches* have they built before?" The answer was *one* and an unorthodox one, at that. Or, rather, Orthodox, Greek Orthodox, a glittery gold-domed Greek church in the middle of a California junkyard. The budget and the setting posed a riddle that leaders find enlivening, an opportunity to touch the landscape in a way that is healing and transformative. That project, like our own, presented a challenge that defied one-size-fits-all solutions.

Looking back on the chance encounter that brought these gifted and edgy architects into my life, I can only come up with the word *grace*. Sure, you can find a thread and trace it back to our unsuccessful attempts to find local designers who were interested both in our building and in our budget.

More than one firm was drawn to the open, mission-minded, peace-loving heart of our congregation. But when they saw our budget—not really enough to build even a custom home—they balked and turned us down.

Thankfully, Joel Barnes, a young church leader with a master's degree in architecture, was chosen to be the chair of the building committee—a task that would last nine years. A preacher's kid, Joel found a team of architects who were eager to put their spades in first. Unable to find a local firm that was a fit, Joel looked to the architecture department at the University of California at Berkeley to find architects who were schooled in "ego-less architecture" and a "timeless way of building." Tall Poppy leaders call on the help they need to carry the vision.

So, they came from the west coast and started with a ten-acre section of Kansas prairie. Their goal was to bring something out of the ground that embellished the contours of the earth, a reflection of and an inspiration for a visionary church family. They camped on the property so they could feel the sun on their faces when they first woke and check the breeze and how it stirred—or didn't—during various times of the day. They set up ladders here and footstools there to sense how creating a berm or lowering the land would change the sacred feel of the site.

What they were trying to imagine, standing tall on their ladders, was something beyond tract housing designed to last fifteen years. The big-box stores with acres of concrete on every corner and the cookie-cutter, consumer-pushing world didn't nourish their spirits, or ours. Until we heard the architects articulate it, we hadn't named it for what it was: a *soul-less* way of building and, ultimately, living. It is a way that begins not with a considered response to the native prairie grass or a bow to the craft of the carpenter, but with one goal: maximizing profits, pushing more and more consumption, encouraging more and more sprawl—with little thought of ways to sustain communities and environments.

What they were trying to create by spending the day in silence, walking the property with their survey stakes and marking the spots where the land felt most alive, where the view of the valley was most pleasing, was something sacred, holy, eternal. As Gary asked our building committee—for a moment like a captivated class—what is it about a hilltop village in Italy, founded fifteen centuries ago, that continues to call the pilgrim? What is it in the winding cobblestone path that beckons young and old to explore?

Timeless. That was the type of architecture they sought—a style of architecture that embodied our faith: lasting, genuine, and organic. It was groundbreaking yet strangely familiar to our ears. It was hope for new heaven, new earth. We paused and reflected and imagined. Timelessness. This, we decided, was our common vision. Tall Poppy leaders take time to make sure the vision encompasses different perceptions. No leader can carry the vision alone; it requires the strength and contribution of the whole community. In this case, that meant our church taking leaps of faith to pave the way for the community we envisioned. It happened because leadership means seeing things differently, and a Tall Poppy vision assumes all perspectives.

Antjie Kroc grew up, as did all whites in South Africa, in a position of unquestioned dominance. Her career, as a writer and journalist, spans the volatile decades before and after the fall of apartheid—the system of brutal separation that kept the black majority under white minority rule for 350 years, until 1992. Nelson Mandela was released from prison that February and was elected the first president of that free country in 1994. Mandela's challenge as the first leader of a newly free country was daunting. Take a highly privileged minority group, educated at exceptional schools, afforded every opportunity, and mix that group in with the enslaved masses—deprived of every opportunity and right. You cannot have a new country overnight, but you can have a Tall Poppy. Nelson Mandela was such a leader.

Kroc writes of the challenge of creating a rainbow nation in a deeply divided land. The title of her book, *A Change of Tongue* (Johannesburgh: Random House, 2003), speaks to the fundamental nature of the transformation that was needed. From the Latin, *trans* means "across," "other side," and *form* means "to give structure to, create, bring forth." To transform is literally to *form the other*; it is how a Tall Poppy first starts creating a new vision. That's part of the leader's responsibility and a step in which Nelson Mandela excelled.

Tall Poppies Lead in Uncertain Times

But the ground in which Tall Poppies dig is anything but solid. Bernie Lyon and Dan Moseley's book, *How to Lead in Church Conflict: Healing Ungrieved Loss* (Nashville: Abingdon Press, 2012), is about leading churches toward health. In it, they look to the work of Zygmunt Baumen, who talks about the "liquid times" we live in:

> Interruptions, incoherence, surprise are the ordinary conditions of our life. They have even become real needs for many people, whose minds are no longer fed . . . by anything but sudden changes and constantly renewed stimuli . . . we can no longer bear anything that lasts. (p. 15)

Leaders, who once could count on solid ground under their feet, cannot know for sure what tomorrow will bring. There is no blueprint to follow in our world. We may not be Nelson Mandela, but we can empathize with some of his obstacles and we can look to how he built consensus by emphasizing peace and reconciliation. But we can also learn from Mandela that leadership is costly and potentially dangerous. Leaders are often vulnerable because they are more visible in leading change. My friend and mentor Kris Culp, a theologian at the University of Chicago Divinity School, explored these truths in *Vulnerability and Glory*. Vulnerability is the hallmark of human existence. We are treasures in earthen vessels. Although by design and nature we are subject to devastation and destruction, we are also meant for glory and transformation despite the uncertainty around us.

Throughout my ministry, I've been graced with mentors who focused on the glory and transformation possible in human life, steeped in God's blessing: "Stand tall. Get out in front. Risk. Dream"; "Unless you are attempting something you have not already mastered, you will never grow"; "When you die, the Holy One will not ask you, why weren't you Moses, but why weren't you Holly?" For whatever reason, while building that church, I was called to be a Tall Poppy. Am I always the tall one? No. But for whatever plan or reason God had in mind, I was it for the moment. And with God's help, I planned to be the best leader I could be.

Being First Has Risk and Reward

Cliché? Yes, but still true. Leaders put their spades in first, and they get attention for it. There is notice, notoriety, and a newsworthy factor that comes from being new, fresh, novel, the "first." Innovation is its own reward. The first one gets the attention and the accolades. Some of that is placement or timing or the simple luck of being in the right place at the right time. Everyone knows the name of Neil Armstrong, the first man to walk on the moon. Do you know who was the second? Far better than a boost to your self-esteem is the personal satisfaction that comes from living out of your core, offering your creative gifts to God's world.

> **Vulnerability goes hand in hand with transformation.**

But vulnerability goes hand in hand with transformation. There is a correlation; risk and reward move together. The goal is maximizing the potential payoff and minimizing the threat. Leaders know how quickly new ground can be lost. People can retreat, surrender—even crumple in a heap. Life is ever shifting, and the new ground must be recreated for the new day. Leaders must find ways to be resilient and help others keep their balance in uncertain, anxiety-provoking times. Just like all leaders, Tall Poppies can get cut down. But they also fall farther. So what buffers the inevitable falls? The will, desire, and spiritual resources to keep putting their spades in buffer the falls because they know what they can bring when they stand up tall—something different, new, fresh.

Consider Sonia Sotomayor as a Tall Poppy. If it hadn't been for this risky quip in 2002—"I would hope that a wise Latina woman with the richness of her experiences would more often than not reach a better conclusion than a white male who hasn't lived that life"—her confirmation to the Supreme Court would have been a complete rubber stamp. To be fair, she wasn't saying this applied to all cases. She had counted up the low, low number of women and people of color who serve as judges—most are white men—and she was speaking about cases involving sex and race discrimination. This statement is not unlike that of Senator John McCain, who said about cases involving prisoner abuse and treatment of detainees, "I would hope that a person with the richness of my experiences (someone detained for years as a prisoner of war) would more often than not reach a better conclusion than someone who hasn't lived that life."

I agree with Sotomayor and McCain: our experiences are unique, special, and extraordinary, at least to us. I'm a white woman. At least once a week, I'm aware of my whiteness and the privileges it brings me. I remember growing up in Texas and being in second grade and seeing the way the black kids were treated when our school was integrated. I also remember thinking, "I am so glad I am not black. So many doors would be shut." But when I graduated from seminary in 1987, some doors were shut because I am a woman. I was at the top of my class. Yet, while my male colleagues traveled the country meeting with search committees, my phone did not ring. My friends Misty and Cheryl even bought me one of the first answering machines; we were sure churches were calling and I was away when the calls came. They weren't. But such experiences made me who I am today and fueled my passion to be a pastor.

As a successful pastor with a growing church, I was designated as a Tall Poppy by my denomination. Things were going well, so I thought. I was even selected to preach at my denomination's national meeting. And then I went home to learn that there were people ready to cut me down. Being a Tall Poppy in our denomination didn't matter to them; they had other plans, and my leadership was not to be a part of their future. Fortunately in the spring before the demand was made for my resignation, I began meeting with consultant Dennis Sweeny. Dennis works with leaders who want to grow their mission to the next level. A refreshing mix of candor, swagger, and heart, Dennis's style is encouraging and challenging. So he was there for me when I was cut down. His advice was different from anyone else's: don't apologize. Stand your ground. You are a leader. Of course you use salty language sometimes, and that's what leaders do. That's why people come to hear you preach. You are authentic, honest, bold. Then he gave me this task: write a statement of beliefs and present it to the church leadership. Tell them, clearly, "This is who I am. This is how I'm going to lead."

Here is what I wrote. It read in part:

Statement of Beliefs

I am proud of what I have built at Saint Andrew Christian Church. It is a congregation unique not only to the area, but to the region and the denomination. I have given twenty-one years of my life, my family, my heart and soul to build it.

I am not perfect. Far, far from it. I never claim to be; that is what people appreciate most about me: my honesty and vulnerability. I stand before the congregation Sunday after Sunday and shine the light on my innumerable imperfections and, more importantly, how our imperfections are nothing when compared to the unfathomable power of God's healing and grace.

I am a strong leader and a deeply committed pastor.

In the end, some members of the church wanted to go in a different direction without my leadership. My vision did not coincide with that of a slim but forceful majority of the leadership circle. I was asked to leave. It was a shattering, searing loss—far deeper than any I've ever sustained. It was devastating for me, my children, and so many in the congregation. I weighed just over 90 pounds when the three-month ordeal ended; I was losing more than my body, I was losing my soul and my mind from the trauma and the grief. So many relationships were lost—hundreds and hundreds—without a single chance to say good-bye or to bring closure. From the young, blessed and baptized, to the old, tended and buried, the vast majority of my relationships were gone—suddenly, inexplicably, cruelly. Looking back, it seems that some actually wanted to mow me down permanently. Some probably thought I deserved it. Had I been too tall, or did people perceive me looking down at them? Were the risks worth the benefits? Yes, because I stood tall not just for myself, but for the weak, the last, the left-out, and the lost. It was time to move on. It wasn't about me anyway. It was about plowing the ground for God's new creation. For me, it was time to carry my spade elsewhere and turn over new soil.

Tall Poppy Leaders Have Confidence

Leaders believe in themselves. Leaders put their spades in first because they have confidence in what they bring to the table. Leaders stand tall because they believe in themselves and believe in their vision. With God's help, they are not afraid of the future. They have come to focus on what is ahead and what is important. They know it. They can see it. They are going for it. But they also stand up for others. I think of Robert Kennedy encountering Americans who were among the most destitute and dispossessed, living in squalor and abject poverty, in the Mississippi Delta. This tall leader called our country to atone and to change through his challenging words, "Some men see things as they are and say 'why?' I dream things that never were and say 'why not'?"

Leaders stand up for others, not over them.

Leaders put their spades in first because they have a vision that is compelling and propelling—focus. It's not based on transience, causing a person to drift from one thing to another. Focus is necessary because we each play a part in God's grand design. If we do our part well, someone else is free to do his or her part well and not worry about ours.

Where does this confidence come from? It comes from a strong spiritual life of prayer, study, and service. It comes from finding mentors and other Tall Poppies who can be there for us in times of distress. It comes from a willingness to learn from mistakes and a familiarity with our own limitations. But mostly it comes from not being afraid and putting our trust in God and God's vision for us all.

Tall Poppy Leaders Keep the Vision

Leaders keep the vision before them. Vision is, as Walter Brueggemann wrote in *The Prophetic Imagination* (Minneapolis: Fortress Press, 2001), offering an alternative consciousness to the dominant consciousness of the world around us, an alternative image of what life in God's beloved community looks like. Where the world says tribalism, scarcity, and war, the faithful say inclusion, abundance, and peace. The vision grows out of the faithful tasks of criticizing/revisioning and energizing. We see these tasks many times in the Bible, from Moses and Miriam to the prophets to Jesus of Nazareth. The Moses saga begins in the movement of slavery to freedom; the slaves cry out; they groan under their bondage; and God hears their cry. Crying, grieving, and criticizing in a plaintive voice—things are not as they should be. It means cutting through the numbness, the death, and denials of our lives and our world. Crying out is the march to Selma, the Montgomery bus boycott, sitting down at a lunch counter in Greensboro, and refusing to be a part of the cover-up in our lives, from our lifeless relationships to our addictive behavior. Tall Poppy leaders learn this as they learn about the vulnerabilities that come from the deepest place within their spirit, the deep waters.

Tall Poppy leaders stand tall, but they go down deep, beneath the surface; they know their story, their self-interest, their fears and insecurities. Their roots hold the soil and draw nourishment from the depths. Those roots work the soil, breaking up clods of grief and pain but also drawing resources to the surface—hopes, longings, dreams. This is Miriam with the tambourine, leading the former slaves as they dance and sing. It is doxology, thankfulness, dreaming of the Promised Land, and the lion and the lamb lying down together.

> **Tall Poppies hold on with deep roots.**

Crying out is tough, but to keep dreaming, imagining, and hoping can be even tougher. As Brueggemann says, we live in a world that can implement anything and imagine nothing. Vision comes from breaking through the tough ground that keeps us stuck in the same old place: the same petty squabbles but also the same military spending, the same suburban sprawl, the same violence and cruelty. Tall Poppy Leaders are done with the "same old"; they have a vision of what can be, and they seize it.

I had almost skipped the retreat for the Planned Parenthood board I served on. We were always under attack from the religious right and conservative politicians and were stuck, understandably, in a defensive posture. The consultant hired for the retreat began: "You've got to turn this around; there is only one way: you have to stay on message. Stay focused on the things you stand for: health care, justice for all, freedom. Americans are with you. Maybe not the vocal minority, but Americans are with you. When they put a microphone in your face and swipe at you, you can't react.

You have to stay on your core message." He passed out bold markers and blank sheets of paper with strings tied through the tops—signs to wear around our neck: "What are your core values? Write down the top four. What's the first thing you'd die for and the last thing you'd give up? Write those four on your sign and put it around your neck. Every day, get up and say: Is that what I'm about today? It's not enough to know what you are against. You have to know: this is what I'm for, and this is what I'm absolutely committed to."

Tall Poppy leaders have core values that become manifest in the vision. Susan Everson, a professor, consultant, and mentor, told our staff at Peace Church, "There is a difference between mission and vision. Most organizations can tell you about their mission: to feed hungry people. But vision—a world where no child is hungry—that's tougher. That's what holds us back." The vision is what leaders keep before the people. And it comes from shared core values.

Not Just Any Vision

Leaders have a vision that is compelling and propelling. One of my favorite passages comes from Barbara Kingsolver's *Animal Dreams: A Novel* (New York: HarperCollins, 1990). In it, Hallie tells her sister why she went to Nicaragua to work for peace:

> Here's what I've decided. The very least you can do in your life is find out what you hope for. And the most you can do is live inside that hope. Not admire it from a distance but live right in it under its roof. What I want is so simple

Leaders Put Their Spades in First

I almost can't say it: elementary kindness. Enough to eat, enough to go around. The possibility that kids might one day grow up to be neither the destroyers nor the destroyed. That's about it. Right now I'm living in that hope running down its hallways and touching the walls on both sides. (p. 299)

Tall Poppy leaders compel and propel with passion: "Thank you for your sermon. I can tell you are so passionate about it. We sat in the balcony and your passion reached all the way up there"; "My brother-in-law heard you speak at the rally; he said you were great, so passionate." Underneath the comments, sadly, was surprise. Folks don't expect passion in the preaching of mainline Protestant pastors. They expect it in television preachers and football coaches, but not in the average church preacher. Our passion can get buried, pushed down, deeper and deeper into the earth until it just goes away.

When you see it, it sticks with you. I remember a concert several years ago. Robert Kapilow, a musician, composer, and scholar of classical music, was in Kansas City to teach kids about classical music. He was so unbelievably passionate, animated, enthusiastic, you almost had to peel him off the ceiling of the Folly Theater. His passion was infectious; even I found myself excited about the cello solo, too.

In the first few months of Peace Christian Church, Joe Hatley—president of our board of trustees—and I talked about the need for close attention to every detail in the bylaws of my new church's foundation. Reflecting on the pain of the recent past and the promise of the future, he said: "We don't want you to lose your passion. We don't want anything to happen to you. That's why we are taking so much time on these bylaws. That's why everyone is being so careful. Not because we don't trust you or the other staff. We do. We love your passion and your intensity. That's why people come. That's why people follow you." Passion gives the urgency for people to act on the vision, *now*.

Tall Poppy leaders have the gift of urgency. It is similar to impatience but different. They are not satisfied with the current state of affairs. What passions do you have? What excites you about the faith? If you can't supply a ready answer, you need to seriously consider where you are in your ministry. Majora Carter is a modern-day prophet. She doesn't fit the stereotype of an environmentalist—a white guy with hiking boots, khaki shorts, and a broad-brimmed hat. No, an African American, Majora grew up in the Bronx and looks like a movie star. She founded an innovative nonprofit corporation called Sustainable South Bronx in 2001 to address pollution and poverty and the unmistakable connection between the two. Children who grow up near trash dumps, brown fields, power plants, and transportation infrastructure suffer from asthma and fall behind their peers in school. By 2005, she had earned a coveted MacArthur "genius" Fellowship.

When Majora came to Kansas City, she started her talk with this question: "Americans are 5 percent of the world's population, and we are 25 percent of the *what*?" The audience guessed: greenhouse gases, consumption of the earth's resources, energy use. She said, "All of the above are true, but they are not the answer I'm looking for. We have 5 percent of the world's people and 25 percent of the world's *prisoners*. One out of four people in the world who is behind bars is in America." Anyone can see that something is out of line. Have a passion for prison ministry? For kids? For issues related to pollution? Or poverty? Look at your immediate environment because the best time is *right now*.

Majora's organization built some of New York City's earliest green roofs, award-winning parks and greenways, green-collar job training and placement systems first, and then built the coalitions to pass policies based on those projects. For Majora, the future of our grandchildren starts with how we treat ourselves, now.

Vision Is about Today

Leaders put their spades in first because they know anything worth doing is worth doing today. I preached at my new church five days after I was dismissed from the previous one. My sense of urgency was acute. I was let go without a dime of severance. Attorneys and advisors close to me assumed I'd get something, at best twenty-one months for twenty-one years of service, or at least twenty-one weeks. I founded the church, built it, and worked ninety-hour weeks for many of those years. I didn't get anything—no severance and, of course, no unemployment. The mortgage, bills to pay, and two teenagers to put through college give you a sense of urgency.

But financial concerns weren't behind the urgency. It was, rather, the need to worship. During the investigation of the grievance filed against me, I was put on leave. I'd been out of worship, the sanctuary, and had not preached for six weeks—the longest stretch in my twenty-five years of ministry. My soul needed a home. I couldn't go another six weeks, not even six days, without a worshiping community. Personally, my vision grows out of my call to preach. I was done sitting on the bench. What about your call? What vision, what passion grows out of your call to ministry? If you really want to be an effective leader, you need to recharge and regroup now. If God called you, God also gave you a vision for ministry.

Leadership Is about the Long Term

Leaders put their spades in first, but they also know that they will have to stay with it for as long as it takes. They believe in the vision. Martin Luther said there were actually three miracles in the birth of Jesus. The first was that God became human; the second was that a virgin conceived; and the third was that Mary believed. He went on to observe that the greatest of these miracles was the last—that Mary believed. Without that, the rest doesn't matter. Leadership can take building and rebuilding relationships for a long time. It takes stamina, but the vision beckons us onward. We run the good race. We believe in the vision we receive. This does not mean that we don't stop and reevaluate from time to time, adjusting the course, taking new soundings of the deep waters. But it does mean that once the adjustments are made, we continue pressing toward the goal.

Take Susan B. Anthony and the other women suffragists. Gail Collins described the years before women won the right to vote as a "seventy-year slog" ("My Favorite August," *New York Times* [August 13, 2010]). When the movement leaders realized that they'd never get past the United States Senate, they knew they'd have to get every state to pass an amendment granting women the right to vote. During the seven decades leading up to the victory, there were some nine hundred campaigns aimed at state legislatures, political parties, and houses of Congress. As Susan B. Anthony said, the great day is "coming sooner than most people think." This is a great line, as Collins said, especially since Anthony said it in 1895, twenty-five years before women got the right to vote.

Tall Poppy leaders believe in the call they've received from God; they know they were created in God's image to offer their gifts. From this deep center, they stand tall. Their clear vision is fueled by passion and momentum: seize this day. They believe. They act.

Architect Gary Black is the tallest man I know. Not just tall. Lanky, with long arms that move around in big arches when he is talking about a project he is passionate about, which would be every project he signs on for, from the homeless shelter in San Jose to the high school in Japan to the sanctuary in Kansas. Gary is a genius and a target. He has been sued, attacked, defamed, derailed, and ridiculed. He has never made much money; he raised his five children with his wife in a small home. But that didn't make much difference to Gary. In a world filled with mediocrity, in which people give themselves to such small things, he's not living for what other people think or offer. Nope, he's shaped his life around what he sees standing on a ladder in the middle of a piece of property in a suburb of Kansas City.

From the very first gathering, our small but hearty half dozen decided just to live as if the church we wished for was a given. Although the next twenty years would have more than their share of conflict over the "issues" of the day, most days we lived, unapologetically, as a congregation that welcomed everyone—gay, straight, and in between. We were a church for which caring for the earth and feeding kids was just part of the expectation, for which sharing openly and with respect for sometimes-conflicting visions was the norm.

Conclusion

So it went. People were taking swipes at me. I've found myself in that same position—somehow attracting attention and attack—all of my life. It's tricky, though, because only when you stand tall and stretch high, only when you attempt things you have not done before, only then will you grow. My first church was deeply planted with spadework from a lot of people, but, for me, it also carried my deepest hopes and longings.

When a new church committee asked me to plant a church in Olathe, Kansas, in 1990, I really had no choice.

I wish I could say it was faith that forced me to say yes. No, it was the lack of other creative and promising options. As a woman pastor, frankly, they were few and far between. So, after six months of hemming and hawing, I gave in and went, drawn by a new vision, with God beckoning me forward.

A tall but *proud* poppy? No, a Tall Poppy by the grace of God. The lessons I learned came at a significant cost. New ground can be lost. At times people retreat, surrender, throw in the towel. Life can shift quickly, and the new ground must be recreated for the new day. What doesn't kill you will make you stronger. God hears the cry of the afflicted; I know because God heard mine.

> **Tall Poppies do the difficult spadework to accomplish goals for the community.**

Starting over. Tall Poppies do that, too. It's never too late. Do you need to reinvigorate your church, yourself? Want to be a better leader? Where do you start? Listen to God's calling, know your core values, keep the vision before you, locate your passion, compel and propel others as you bring them on board, learn from the hard lessons, and grow into the image God has for you. For if you do these things, you will know where to put your spade, and you will also see that the Promised Land is on the horizon.

chapter two

Leaders Build

Dennis was drawing a diagram on a napkin. I was taking notes, thinking, "This guy is sharp."

He said, "So a leader is up on top of the light pole—looking out, surveying, seeing the possibilities up front. Seeking new business, new ventures, new places to expand; or else you become stale. And then you have to have a person, stable, on the ground, running the operations: the day-to-day stuff . . ."

He was talking fast, and I was writing fast.

"And then, you need a creative team with synergy and passion—and a high level of trust."

Trust? I put my pen down. A high level? Hmmm . . . it hit a nerve, one I didn't even know was so raw and exposed. Trust? The word didn't fit the current staffing situation at the church that I had founded twenty-one years earlier. He was right on, of course, painfully so. Trust is absolutely necessary to a staff, a congregation, a board of trustees, a thriving company, a group of mountain climbers.

It's right there below the other must-haves necessary for a healthy team, as described through the research and writings of Carl Larson and Frank LaFasto (*Teamwork: What Must Go Right and What Can Go Wrong* [Sage Publications, 1989]).

Teams need:

- a clear, elevating goal—something that makes you look up and out
- structures that are results driven
- a competent team

and then this fourth one:

- intense, unified commitment

Intense, unified commitment.

Tall Poppy Leaders Build Teams Who Trust

Effective teams are dedicated to the endeavor and to one another. I realized this, too late, when my church imploded. We had established congregational teams that were targeted, functional, and effective, for the most part; but there were some key areas and critical elements—such as performance evaluations and candid feedback—that were missing. And as the leader of the church, I bore much of the responsibility for these missing pieces.

If you want teams that are highly creative and synergetic, that just won't do. Thriving, fluid organizations need teams with a high level of trust, honesty, and respect, and that must start at the top. Before I started my second church, I started such a team, a worship team. I couldn't live without it and I knew it.

> **Tall Poppy leaders must build trust first.**

Far and away, the most soul-wrenching part of losing the church I had founded was losing the worship service I had created and refined. The worship service was rich and spirited, toe-tapping and soul-feeding. No one needed it like I needed it. I also lost the gift of the rhythm of weekly preaching and worship. For the better part of twenty-five years, my life had repeated the same tune: reading scripture early in the week, working through the text while on my daily run, and then preaching. Without that structure, I found it hard to stand tall and conduct, to be inspired, to sing. As the minister in this new place, I needed to preach in a community steeped in rich, spirited worship. I needed a team, a team I could trust, a team who would have my back, one who could stand behind me while I led. Frankly, I needed a team in which I felt safe to explore new possibilities without having to worry or glance over my shoulder. I thought of Eli Chamberlain and Alex Holsinger, two gifted singers and people of deep, open, honest, loyal, and progressive faith. The sound they create can only be described as amazing grace. From traditional hymns to world music to folk, from the songs of the Dixie Chicks to Bruce Springsteen, they filled the heart and the room with their hope-filled, justice-seeking faith. If I find a place to preach, I asked them, can you sing?

"I'm all in," Eli said, and Alex, too.

"I'm all in."

And from everyone who joined our new church: "I'm all in."

When John Jordan stepped up to lead the choir—expanding the repertoire, size, and strength of the music team—we knew we were on our way.

"We're all in."

We had found our next lyric.

We had "teams" in place before we were a church—

a worship team,

music team,

service team,

mission team, peace-making team, environmental team, children/youth team, bylaws team, finance team—committed teams and crucial building blocks for our song.

Leaders Build Commitment with Gratitude

After trusting teams comes commitment. I hear that commitment over and over in shared words and shared actions of our church members, like in the thoughtful card that came in the mail from a sixty-five-year-old woman who attended Peace Church. I put it with others in a box under my bed. I take them out and read them for inspiration and encouragement.

It began with a word of gratitude for a pastoral visit. Then she wrote *I come with full commitment to Peace Church*. She added a few lines—about her family, faith, journey—then repeated it: *I come with full commitment to Peace Church*. And, a third time: *my husband and I have come with full commitment*.

We are committed to the purpose, committed to your leadership.

Leaders build relationships. Leaders build teams, teams with unified commitment. To-die-for commitment is grounded in gratitude. That's what you find in the story of Ruth. Naomi and her husband are in Bethlehem—*beyit lechem*, the house of bread—but there is no bread, only famine. They head to Moab where their sons marry foreign women, Ruth and Orpah. The men die, and the three women are left in a vulnerable place. Naomi chooses to head home, for protection and provision. When her daughters-in-law follow, Naomi tells them to return to their homeland. They persist, and, again, Naomi resists. Then come the famous words, spoken between Ruth and Naomi, daughter-in-law to mother:

> But Ruth said, "Do not press me to leave you / or to turn back from following you! / Where you go, I will go; / where you lodge, I will lodge; / your people shall be my people, / and your God my God. / Where you die, I will die— / there will I be buried. / May the LORD do thus and so to me, / and more as well, / if even death parts me from you!" (Ruth 1:16-17)

The words are standard fare at weddings and holy unions; in truth, though, they express what every team needs—to be "all in." That's what you want, whether the team you are a part of is a couple, a family, a congregation, or a campaign.

But there is more to glean from Ruth's story. No shrinking violet, Ruth doesn't wait around for a guy to ask her to dance. She washes and anoints herself, goes to the threshing room floor where the well-to-do Boaz is lying down, uncovers him, and so it goes. Boaz steps up and makes a legal commitment to Ruth. A baby is born to the unlikely couple. It is a story of passion, fruit, abundance—but not just for these two. From their son's line will come King David and, as the Gospels proclaim, Jesus of Nazareth. It's the commitment of the various people in the story that brings life to the family and to the community and, eventually, to the entire creation.

Leaders build on the foundation of commitment.

Tall Poppy leaders build commitment, and they build on it—creating an environment in which grateful people want to broaden and share their talents, where people feel enough trust to offer their best selves.

Talented and disciplined, Eli Chamberlain and Alex Holsinger said "yes" to our church before it was a church, when we were "just" a worshiping community, before we were

Peace Christian Church. As they assumed the leadership role in our worship service, their contributions expanded exponentially, their rich voices became even clearer, their passion for our new church became more profound, and their faith deepened. The congregation followed.

Strong Leaders Invite Help to Build

Strong leaders invite help—and lots of it. I learned this lesson the tough way, losing a call where I'd been the Tall Poppy leader for years. Putting pushing forward with dogged determination, even when others disagreed, had worked to a point. The church—an open, progressive, mission-driven community—had grown to six hundred in worship on Sundays and a $1.3 million budget. My leadership style was collaborative at times, but, at others—when the stakes were high and I was sure I was "right"—I could lead in a unilateral and impatient and, at times, dismissive manner.

Shortly after that call ended, a denominational leader who had served as a mentor and colleague came to town and took me to lunch, encouraging me to reach out, again, and start another new congregation. "Holly, you are a racehorse. That's how you are built. And if you go to "First Church" here or "First Church" there, they will try and put a harness on you and make you into a workhorse. They'll try and break your spirit."

He was right, of course. I am a racehorse. The one thing universally acknowledged about me is my energy level and my speed. His words also underscored a weakness in my style: folks appreciate my passion, spunk, and spirit, to a point; but they can also find it dizzying, exhausting, disorienting, unsettling, and sometimes overwhelming.

Racehorses need to be reined in. If their instincts are unchecked, they will run at a breakneck pace from the instant the race starts, exhausting themselves long before the finish line. They need steady jockeys to slow them down at times, to pace them, and to pounce to the lead when the right opportunity presents itself. Like people, racehorses need boundaries, guidance, and rest. Their accomplishments and their careers can be vastly extended, not just by a harness, but by a team of handlers who pull together toward a goal.

In my first new church start, I came out of the blocks sprinting. With the exception of sabbatical and study time, for most of the twenty-one years, I'd run as fast as I could, which is pretty fast as a committed marathoner of slight build. After the conflict erupted, my friend Kris Culp wrote me words that were not enough to save that call but that guided me in the establishment of Peace Christian Church:

> The heart of this crisis is not finally about you. It's about the church: about stress in holding together lives in a rough economic climate, about the need for security and control.
>
> In the long run, some "routinization of charisma" (sociologist Max Weber's term) by way of stronger lay leadership and clearer lay patterns of authority

should help level out this backlash by channeling and spreading authority that was centered in you to congregational structures. Or to put it a little differently, folks need to have other than yes Holly/no Holly options or Holly/other staff options.

The increased role of leadership in this crisis could move the church along. As you've said, it's tricky with a congregational system: perhaps taking some steps toward a presbyterian system but with governance via ethos and communal processes of consent more than a rulebook. Matters of nurturing lay leadership and of enhancing a sense of congregational responsibility take new importance . . . with lay leadership structures and patterns in place, but more of those will help shield you in the future and also afford you some separation and space to continue to pursue high-profile things such as speaking and writing.

She was right. Leaders build teams, resources, and structures to outlast their own tenure. I recognized that I had sometimes truncated this, but now I have a new opportunity to put this learning into better practice. I won't make the same mistake this time around. The extra time it takes "up front" to build a team *who builds a church* is an investment in the short run and the long run. People support that which they create. If you build it, they will come; but if *they* build it, they will come back. Although I had put this truth into action most days, I didn't do it every day. This time in this church, I have wise, persistent voices, like the president of our board of trustees, who insist on carefully creating structures that require a team effort.

> **Strong leaders know they need help.**

If Susan Everson said it once, she said it a thousand times: we need a board that clearly understands what belongs to the board. If our president said it once, he said it a thousand times: "Holly, what we're trying to do here takes time, but it's important. We need bylaws that are carefully crafted; we are trying to prevent a future blowup by clearly defining the roles of the lay leaders and the staff but then forcing them to work together as a team to accomplish the church's objectives. We each have strengths to bring to the table, and by complementing our talents, rather than letting one person try to do it all, we each have responsibility for the church's success or failure." People who build something up are far less likely to destroy it.

Tall Poppy Leaders Listen and Collaborate

Unless the event is a short sprint—or a task that needs to be done very quickly—a team can out-perform an individual. Wise leaders know this. Like the elders who helped Moses keep his arms in the air, committed laity are invaluable. With rare exception, and then only in the short run, a lone-ranger leader cannot address a complex, challenging task, especially when it involves multiple people, resources, and systems. Therefore, Tall Poppy leaders build trusting teams across diverse disciplines to accomplish a call.

Trust. Shared purpose. Commitment. Collaboration. Leaders have the opportunity to build teams, resources, and missions and extend the possibilities that come from a shared vision and common values.

Building Is a Process

"We will interview a dozen foundation guys," the architect, Gary Black, said. "And one of them, hopefully, will get it. What we are trying to do here, which has never been done before, is create something sacred, holy, amazing from the stuff they make sewers and highways out of—just concrete. But, the way we use it, the way we pour it into these great columns, the way we apply it, is really, really beautiful." What they were after, I'd figure out, was not a product, again, but a process. A process, as far from modern building practices as you could get; not the assembly-line, soul-less slapping up of drywall in one house after another and moving on, but rather, a process that took a team of passionate people and brought them together to build a unique and soul-stirring structure.

They began with the inherent belief in the creative potential of each person. The idea that at the human core was the desire to create, to contribute, to offer what is true and just—*that* is at the heart of who we are. It's a way of building—and living—in the world that has almost been lost.

Listening to them, I thought of an article I'd read years before about depression and addiction found in the autoworkers on an American assembly line, who performed the same monotonous task for eight hours a day, five days a week. The industrial psychologists had been struck by the disparity they found in the health of those American workers compared to the better health of European workers, who worked in a plant where a car was constructed, from the first bolt to the last, by a *team* of five. The cost of how we live is so high and often so invisible.

So they were on the lookout for a carpenter with a twinkle in his eye, one who would see the plans and smile, the concrete contractor who would say, "I've waited my whole life for a project like this."

It made sense to me.

Relationships Are the Ways and Means

People. They are the heart and soul of leadership. Although I confess to stretching myself too thin at times, I've always strived to know the names of everyone who comes to my church, whether they are regular members or infrequent guests. But before their names, I want to know their stories.

> People, not money, are the ways and means.

Folks ask me, how do you remember so much about people? My only answer is, "I care." And I work at it. You meet someone and you take a second to really look at the person and repeat her name. Or, after worship, you go back through the attendance book and mark the people you just preached to. That process, which might take a half-hour when your brain is still fresh, is worth five hours later in the week. You can see the young mother going out the church door, who is attending for the second time, who mentioned last week that her husband just moved out. You notice the way she looks—the stress, the grief, the "how in the heck am I going to manage" look on her face.

People support that which they create. It's an old proverb that you find across cultures and continents: from the African proverb, "Those who build the building are built by it," to the words attributed to Winston Churchill, "At first we build our buildings, thereafter they build us."

While most Americans can quote the line from the movie *Field of Dreams*, "If you build it, they will come," the truth is, when you are a local church pastor or a leader of any organization, what you want is more than just having them "come." What you want is for folks to get fully engaged, to make connections, to contribute their creativity, passion, and resources. You want people who will reach out in mission and ministry for the long haul.

This is the goal of Tall Poppy leadership—creating and sustaining sacred community. The process will take time, but the rewards will be far richer and more grace-filled than you can imagine.

It was a tough time for me, August of 1993, three years after I started Saint Andrew. I had envisioned an ambitious timeline when I went to new church training in June of 1990; there were ten new church plants represented at the training, and ultimately, only two survived. Starting a new church is far from a sure bet. On that timeline, I pictured a groundbreaking service in 1992, with a move into the building in 1993. Sure enough, we pulled together a building team in 1992, but we finally dedicated our sanctuary in June of 1999. In large part, the church was simply too progressive for the community, significantly so. In part, new church ministry is simply daunting—and liable to fail.

In late 1992, when our building fund had reached the grand total of $972, I decided to try the "friends of the zoo" fund-raising approach. We would reach out to our family and friends, foundations interested in eco-friendly building projects, and other individuals whom we knew supported a wide range of progressive causes. There was only one thing that was on "schedule" according to the timeline: I was pregnant. But I had a miscarriage over the fourth of July weekend while I was alone in Kansas City. My husband was with my parents in New Mexico looking at property. My regional minister (who served as my pastor) had gone with my husband, too. It was the time before cell phones and e-mail. My two close friends, both pastors, were out of town for the holiday. I remember being in the emergency room, and then preparing for surgery, all alone. I just could not think of who to call.

My family came home, but the feeling of being alone hung on through that fall; the word that comes to mind is *ennui*, or listlessness. It was like I was in a boat, out in the middle of a lake, and nothing was moving, no wind, not the slightest breeze. I remember getting up and going to work every day and coming home—except there wasn't any place to go. I worked out of my home, all day long. I remember thinking: is this all there is, just an endless pile of work?

We had sent out hundreds of letters to foundations, family, and friends. We had received several generous checks but not enough to cover even the architect's initial fees. The money trickled in and then all but dried up. I almost gave up going to the post office box. Then, one day in October, there it was: a big fat envelope from Columbia, Missouri, filled with letters from children along with their vacation Bible school offering. Three churches had held a joint VBS, and Saint Andrew was their "mission" effort. The letter from the pastor said, "Sorry this is so late coming. The kids come in and out of my office, putting their hands on the envelope, praying for your church, asking, "How is Pastor Holly? Saint Andrew Church? Do they have a playground yet?"

There were coins and dollars, amounting to $212. All of that time, I thought I was alone on the lake, and those children had been praying for us. Later, another envelope arrived, from another address I didn't recognize in Seattle, Washington. I had sent hundreds of letters out soliciting funds, but I didn't know anyone there.

Inside was a note from a woman named Dorothy. Earlier that summer she had joined our small church for worship in the school gym. It was a last-minute, out-of-the-blue choice; their plans had changed, and she had noticed our ad in the faith page of the local newspaper. There she found what she was looking for—a church with a woman pastor. At eighty-something, she was a "woman's libber," as she called it. Along with an encouraging letter was a check for $10,000.

I don't know how long I sat in the parking lot crying, staring out into the empty field where one day there would be houses, and folks who would want a church like Saint Andrew. I only know I was knocked to the ground by the grace of God, and then the world began to move again. The breeze began to blow, and the life deep within me began to stir; I heard a new song in the wind.

Tall Poppy Leaders Help Build God's Sacred Community

Those two gifts were the sign I needed. Leaders build resources; they sow and scatter, and then they gather the fruits, small and large. They come together to build God's sacred community. Ultimately, our multifaceted approach worked; a wondrous sanctuary was blessed, albeit nine years after the congregation began. In the meantime, we had spent almost a decade worshiping in a school gym.

It began, though, with truly buying in to the idea that people are important, that they are worth the time, effort, and sacrifice. Leaders create teams, and teams create the future. Effective unified teams form healthy organization; they bring focus, depth, and breadth, and they extend the life of the mission.

It takes more than accomplishment and effectiveness to keep people engaged. People are looking for more. They need meaning, passion, and purpose in God. In an effective team, members function at the top of their creative potential, moving God's world forward. I think of my close friend and colleague Cindy, a pastor who married a school superintendent. They have functioned as an informal team through their twenty-six years of marriage: consulting, encouraging, challenging. Or I think of Bob and Barbara, professors at a college in Iowa. I asked Bob about a sermon series I was constructing on sexuality. I expected to find a long book in the mail, some dense philosophical responses. Instead he paused, reflected, and said, "I think sexuality can be such a gift, that it's a shame to mess it up." Then he spoke of the grace he's known in forty years with Barbara, his partner and spouse, the self-confidence, the trust, the grace he has known in her arms. Kris Culp underscored that truth in her work on vulnerability and glory. To be vulnerable is to be open to change. We affect one another, influence one another, shape one another.

That's what scholar and writer Audre Lorde spoke of in her essay "Uses of the Erotic." She contrasts *eros*, or the erotic, with pornography. Pornography is feeling and sensation without connection, but the erotic is feeling with deep connection—being in touch with the core, the soul, the deepest part of who you are. Lorde speaks of the rush you feel in the arms of a lover and, more, the rush that comes from writing a poem, bringing in the harvest, marching for a cure with a thousand others.

Lorde speaks about growing up during the Second World War and the rations her family received. They bought sealed plastic packets of white, uncolored margarine. Inside the packet was a pellet of yellow coloring. Her mother would leave the bag out to soften. It was Audre's job to pinch the pellet and break it inside the bag, releasing the yellowness into the soft margarine, taking it carefully between her fingers. She would knead it back and forth, over and over, until the color had spread through the whole pound of margarine. So the erotic is the sacred, holy power within our spirits. When it's released, it brings color and power to our whole lives.

A year into Peace, we initiated a listening campaign—a campaign to have one-on-one listening sessions with every member of the church. Built on a community organizing model, the listening campaign reflects this truth: whether your goal is ending segregated lunch counters or building a strong congregation, it begins with relationships. In community, our sacred, powerful passions are unleashed for God's work in the world.

I think of my colleague and how deeply her ministry is sustained by her marriage. When she turned forty and fell in love with the man who is now her husband, she said, "Oh, this is what God intended." The two are a team, a home, a sanctuary for each other.

Leaders Build the Future with God's Abundance

Leaders build passion, among two, four, six . . . a hundred. As the poet Marge Piercy wrote in "The Low Road," two people, standing back to back, can fight their way through a crowd, "A dozen make a demonstration. / A hundred fill a hall."

To be sure, people often join a church to fulfill their self-interests, even if their self-interests consist of feeling good about what they do for others. Regardless of why people get involved, though, when they become committed to the work of the church, a future opens up for the community. Trust, connection, and enlivenment are gifts that can come to those who work closely together. God's vision is generous and abundant.

I filed for divorce, after twenty-five years of marriage, when Peace Church was three months old. When I shared that decision with the staff on a Monday morning and feared how it would decimate the young congregation, John looked at me and said: "We are here for one another, we are holding one another, and we are pushing forward." The rest of the staff nodded, saying, "You bet, we are all in." When I shared the news with my congregation at the close of worship the following Sunday, Eli followed it with a short statement of unqualified support.

The congregation nodded: "We are here for you and for your family." We are all in. They meant it. Over and over and over, people have held me up. Honestly, before I lost my church and my marriage, I had no idea what it meant to depend on your "teammates." Over the next year I would find myself, time and again, shaking my head in amazement at the staunch, unwavering support of my team members. One member after another carried me.

That's teamwork. A year after I filed for divorce I sat across the table from my pastoral relations team. I shook my head in amazement.

This was the second time I started a new church; I was blessed with wise, seasoned leaders and colleagues who formed a team of unwavering loyalty, unified commitment, passion, and purpose, but there was something else: a willingness to stand up to me and say, "Slow down. With all the change and disruption people have endured, we have to work together this time, and you have to let others carry the load more." I did not always welcome the feedback and input. Sometimes I resented the structures that "slowed me down." Yet, that's how a team, with a unified mission and purpose, can build something together that endures beyond the tenure of a single Tall Poppy leader. Leaders build teams, resources, and structures. Structures extend the mission—beyond us, into the future.

A few people can run across the country, solo. But they will make a bigger impact if they find a hundred people who will follow, even if for just a part of the journey. Sustaining our passion requires an alternative community that differs from the dominant culture. The voice we hear echoed in the media and marketing is one of tribalism, scarcity, war. The message of the gospel is community, abundance, peace. It is only by working together that we can make the gospel real in our own lives.

He was one of the thousands of homeless kids in Guatemala City. Malnourished, he could have been eight years old or maybe fourteen. He came up to the table in the restaurant where a professor was sitting, alone, waiting for her group. She was on a delegation of church women; they'd come to learn about and express solidarity with the people, most of them desperately poor and emerging from years of civil war. The boy, begging, held his hand out. She smiled and shook her head, "No es posible." He stared at her for a minute, and she looked down at her book; he finally walked away.

Five minutes later he returned. He'd been to several more tables and then came back to her, begging. Again she said, "No es posible." He stared harder then held his hand out, firmly, and said, "Sí, *es* posible." He was right, of course. It was possible for her to spare some change.

It was not that she was uncaring, indifferent—far from it. Thoughtful and compassionate, she could see beyond this boy to the five thousand behind him. She could see beyond the hunger of this day, to the next and the next, stretching on. It wasn't possible. It was the same for the disciples gathered on the hillside who wanted to send the five thousand away. They were concerned that it was growing dark and late, but not Jesus. They said to him: what will these folks have to eat? When Jesus answered that the disciples should give them something, they responded: not possible, because they had only five loaves and two fish. These leaders wanted to feed the people. That dream and vision runs from the first page of Luke's Gospel to the last. Remember Mary's song that God has lifted up the poor and Jesus' first sermon, to preach good news to the poor.

Dream. Imagine; that was the invitation that came in the fund-raising letter from Kaw Valley Habitat for Humanity. The request was not for a box of nails, but for the "resurrection of the urban core."

That's not possible. But Jesus believes it is. And because he believes it is, it is. When his team of leaders said they couldn't feed the people, Jesus did not scold them; he gave them a structure, a plan to follow: sit the people down in groups of fifty, and then you can feed them.

Leaders build for others so all will prosper.

Leaders do not feed everyone themselves, but they help build structures that can eventually feed everyone. That's not easily done. It means dismantling current structures that keep the world as it is, from the arms industry to the food industry. That's what leaders do: they build teams, relationships, resources, and structures that make the impossible possible. They rely on trust, gratitude. They build a sacred, even beloved, community with God-given, abundant resources for us all, now and forever.

chapter three

Leaders Find Water Even in the Desert

It is a brutal story. Abraham sent Hagar and Ishmael into the desert wilderness to die. Sarah is in on it, too. She may have even orchestrated it. It is a familiar story of jealousy and betrayal. Sarah's anxiety is piqued when she sees her son, Isaac, playing with Ishmael, the son of Abraham, her rightful husband, and her slave woman Hagar. "He will not inherit with my son," she says and tells Abraham to send them away. Abraham is grieved. It is not just a request to send them to the summer home. Abraham is sending them out into the wilderness. Even with the bit of bread and water, they will die.

Hagar and Ishmael are cast out—alone. At least when Pharaoh cast out the Hebrew slaves, God was on their side. In Hagar's story, God appears to side with the oppressor. Abraham is distressed, but God minimizes the situation: "Ishmael will be OK. I'll give him a nation, too." God distances Ishmael and Hagar. Ishmael is now the "lad" instead of "your son." Hagar is no longer "your wife," but "your slave woman." Hagar is banished with her child in the wilderness, alone; no voice steers her to a spring. The wilderness is arid, alien, a deathbed. Where is God now?

Naming the Desert Place

Leaders know that desert place: a place where our spirits wither, our bodies shrivel and shrink. My childhood friends from Texas have stood by me, steadfast, through the twenty-year challenge of building a church and the challenge of starting over. They have gone before me in every facet of life: ministry, motherhood, marriage. But now, facing a divorce, I looked to Texas again for chips and salsa and sustenance. I had seen one friend go through a divorce, wasting away, quite literally, getting smaller and smaller. I'd seen her search for water, desperate and determined. I'd seen her vulnerable then strong, unsure then certain. But she came through—full, alive, glorious—like a cactus with a yellow bloom standing out against the dry withered earth. But first she had to name the desert in her life. We do, too. But there are also walls.

It was a brutal news story on public radio about the wall. I've seen it: a twenty-eight-feet-tall wall of concrete. The wall divides Israel and the Palestinian territories. The speaker described how difficult it has made daily life for people who have to cross to get to work or to be with family. It is dangerous, too. Since the wall was begun ten years ago, the number of those who die trying to cross has risen from three a year to more than two hundred.

Then I realized: they are talking not about "that" wall, but the wall along the U.S. border with Mexico. Much of it is in the desert. I had just finished reading *The Devil's Highway*, detailing the danger of the journey. For many, the desert becomes the final resting ground. I was so focused on another country's wall that I was not even thinking about our own.

As a native Texan, I had followed the building of the wall some years back. But not lately. I was not even sure what they call it: the Wall? That's one reason the act of naming something is important. Once we name something, we are more likely to notice it and respond appropriately. Whether your child is gifted or developmentally delayed, you name it and *then* you gather resources.

Take the wall in the Middle East. The two sides disagree, not just on the need for the wall, but on what to call it. Israelis call it a security fence. Security is *the* point—to keep suicide bombers out. Palestinians respond that the wall is not about security, but about *separation*, separating Palestinians from one another, separating people from their land and family. They call it a wall of separation.

Naming is important. How we name something shapes how we respond to it—a security fence or a wall of separation. It's true in our lives, too. We have to name the deserts for what they are. Then we can find water, or if the water has dried up, we can move on.

> **Leaders have to name the deserts for what they are.**

Plan to Find the Water

The young leader went first. I was relieved. I didn't want to start calling on the pastors who were meeting for the first—and only—time to share their sabbatical plans. Circled up in the corner of a conference room, the ten were used to leading, carrying the conversation, drawing people out. But the topic in this session was personal. Specifically, the topic was what hope, hurt, longing—thirst—drove the design of their sabbatical grant. They had been sitting for much of the day, listening to a presenter, taking it in. This session was their time to share. I led off with a question, "In a word, or phrase, distill your sabbatical down to a presenting issue."

One of the younger pastors, sharp, successful, grounded, spoke up: "Loneliness. Isolation. In a nutshell, that's what I feel seven years into this call." You could feel the breath that everyone in the group had been holding release as he spoke. They nodded their heads as he described his sabbatical goal: friendship. "Getting in touch with my old friends, reconnecting with the neighbor kids I grew up with, the high school buddies." Like Moses who found water in the desert, he needed to replenish his soul, so he was planning how to do it. You could see it in the faces of the other pastors: thirst, being drained and barren. They were worn down and worn out and were tired of being mowed down by conflict, the daily grind of complaints, the church family who wanted to control and to manipulate. They were in the desert place.

Go Forth

In the ancient days, with no cameras to capture images, they had to rely on language, and repetition was used to underscore a point: *Sarah was barren, she had no child.* Barren comes from the Hebrew word for "rootless," "uprooted," "pulled up and out." The voice comes to Abraham and Sarah: *go forth from your native land . . . to the land that I will show you* (Genesis 12:1). Go forth. When you are thirsty and can't take another step, get up and go.

Even if you go it alone—as the rabbis who translated "go forth" as "go by yourself" understood—there are moments when leaders have to search for water, life, and hope alone. There are some journeys, like dying, that you make on your own. Finally, it is just you before God. But that is not the entire journey. Abraham went forth, taking Sarah, his family, and his servants. Here *go forth* means "go *to* yourself." So Abraham traveled and "came to himself." Perhaps he realized the full extent and consequences of his actions in sending Hagar and Ishmael away. The desert is good for that—coming to yourself. But we need water wherever we are, so *going forth* might mean digging deeper where you are. Or a leader *going forth* might mean taking a sabbatical, finding a new challenge; but it can also mean just keeping moving on.

Where do you need to *go forth*?

My friend Rabbi Amy Katz moved across the country a few years ago to take a position as a senior rabbi. Her leave-taking was nothing like that of the Polish Jews who had no safe place to go. It had none of the uncertainty of Abraham, Sarah, or Hagar; her family left one beautiful home for another. But her journey began like many: the force that propels you to leave has a smidgen of barrenness, a hollow place, a lacking. In the case of clergywomen—rabbis and pastors—the opportunities for women often run out before the women reach their potential.

What makes the journey really tough is getting pulled up by the roots, after building relationships and networks. It's tough on kids, too, which is why most folks want to stay put. Leaders aren't immune to these difficulties. I think of the hydrangea plant in our backyard. It has gorgeous blue flowers. The only problem is it's behind the garage and you can't see it. I asked my friend Kris Culp, a theologian and good gardener, what she thought, "Could I dig it up? Move it?" She replied, "I don't know. After five or six years, the roots go pretty deep. If you are going to move it, do it in the spring, before it's started any leaf development. If you wait until it's flowering, it's really hard for it to survive."

That's the challenge my friend the rabbi faced, moving across the country with her husband and children, with one in high school—it's tough to be uprooted when you are flowering, in the midst of growth. The journey is tough and long, and you have to go deep inside and pull out everything you've got. Tall Poppies have deep roots; reach as deep as possible. Go to your roots, and find the authentic part of who you are.

Some Gifts Can Only Be Had in the Desert

The story of Hagar and Ishmael in the desert is searing, even terrifying. Still, there is grace. In a world of slavery, they are not sold but freed. Hagar and Ishmael leave Abraham's house, not as someone's property, but as emancipated people. Emancipation is not without its challenges, though. They have nothing to eat, and they wander in the wilderness without drink.

Leaders recognize desert places; they know them well. But they have faith that traveling in the desert is not the final destination. The desert wilderness can become a place of blessing and freedom. God hears Hagar and provides a great future. Leaders learn that some gifts can only be had in the wilderness. While Hagar's situation is uncertain, she receives a great gift. God hears her and speaks to her—a lowly outcast. This is a gift that Sarah never experiences.

> **Leaders sometimes hear God's voice in the desert.**

When I served on the Midwest Board for Holocaust Education, I attended a special screening of the film *Defiance*, the true story of the Bielski brothers. In 1941, after the Nazis invaded Belarus, the Jews were forced into ghettos, and later, these were liquidated and the Jews sent to concentration camps. Some people refused to live in the ghetto, such as the Bielskis. With a handful of others, they fled into the forest where they became partisan fighters and resisters. The frozen earth with snow piled high, a bin of potatoes often empty, no medicine to stop the spread of typhus, and the nearing German army meant survival was moment to moment. In a wilderness where death seemed guaranteed, some survived. They made a makeshift camp, and eventually it became more elaborate, with a hundred workers toiling in workshops, tailors patching old clothes, shoemakers making new footwear, and watchmakers learning to repair rifles, and a synagogue, a bakery, and a medical clinic.

But, as they died, starving to death, some grumbled that they wanted to leave the wilderness and go back to the ghetto. The leader, Tuvia, responded: "Anyone who wants to leave can leave, go back to the ghetto, but the forest is the only place in all of Europe where a Jew can live freely. That's what we've chosen, and if we die next year or next week or tomorrow, well, every day is one more day of freedom."

You can't be afraid to move. When I was the pastor of Saint Andrew, we changed locations four times in the first nine years. Sometimes it was out of necessity—the school district moved us—sometimes we moved voluntarily, for a location with more potential and possibility. And every time we moved, we picked up new people. Maybe the state legislators of Kansas were unsure about evolution, but we weren't.

Peace Church is proving to be even more nimble. In one year, we've moved the evening service four times largely for practical reasons—air conditioning, mosquitoes, armed robbery. Beyond the practical, we move because we're not afraid. We are called to it, to be Peace on the move. Our staff motto embodies our freedom and energy: *Scrappy, ready, real.* We are a community on fire with God's peace and justice. We are free, free to catch the spirit.

Leaders Believe They Will Survive

In his book *Deep Survival: Who Lives, Who Dies and Why*, Laurence Gonzales (New York: W.W. Norton & Co., 2003) offers fascinating, harrowing stories of people who survive plane crashes, mountain-climbing accidents, and more. It is an exploration of the thoughts and actions that separate the heroic survivor from the rest. How is a seventeen-year-old girl, with no shelter, food, or equipment, able to survive a plane crash, walking for eleven days out of the Peruvian jungle? Adults, far better equipped, fall down and die. Of all the traits that stand out for me about those who survive, this is the most important: a survivor believes she will survive; she is sure she will, eventually, find water.

Leadership Is a Process

The sabbatical proposals shared a recurring theme: a movement from a scattered, fragmented ministry to a centered, grounded call. When I read a particularly strong and creative proposal, I thought, "Now that is vision; that is leadership—finding water in the desert, going to your roots, finding nourishment not just to survive but to thrive."

Creative and visionary, Saint Gregory of Nyssa in San Francisco has a food pantry with an art center and more. There are folks who love to weave and folks who like to make soup, side by side, holding together beauty and justice. The priest, Paul Fromberg, developed a sabbatical that embodied his passion and imagination. Fromberg wanted to paint traditional images of the Madonna in fresh ways: an earthy, gritty picture of mother and child living on a city dump or out in a field, harvesting.

He designed his sabbatical to go *to* himself, deeply, to go back to his roots, to find what watered his spirit. He wrote about being a ten-year-old boy. Before he was a pastor, he was a painter: "I would invent things that had no purpose other than to be beautiful." It was water in the desert that kept his spirit fresh and his soul full.

That's what the architects were looking for on our church property and in our souls when they came from California to Kansas to build Saint Andrew's sanctuary: our deepest longings, our wildest hopes, our truest selves, the place where we, as individuals and as a community, bear and become the presence of God. Before they stood on the property, they met with me and the building chair. It was late in the evening—close to eleven our time—but the night was still young on their west coast. We sat for hours, talking, while they listened: "Tell us about you. Your church. We've seen your mission statement, your concern for peace with justice, your desire to move beyond conflict. Tell us about your worship service. What time do people arrive? What happens when they pull up in their car to the school gym where you worship? Do people set up chairs? Make coffee?" They pulled out their sketchbooks and began writing: lots of talking, children running, everyone helping.

After just a few hours of sleep, they were back at it, this time with an expanded group—the building committee. They were quite a sight. One, Cullen, was young and gorgeous. The leader, Gary Black, was tall, lanky, and had sparkling eyes underneath a broad-brimmed hat that went with the long sleeves, a sign of too much sun as a kid and a run-in, already, with cancer. The third would be with us only a while before life and a longing for the native, the home, the authentic, would take Kyriakos back to his village on the Greek isle of Cyprus.

I thought of the interview with the architects a few months before. I had shown up for the conference call a bit tired, drained. I was holding my one-month-old baby on my lap, nursing her, as I shouted over the speakerphone: "Tell us about your understanding of sacred space" (after all, they had just completed their one church building, a Greek Orthodox church adjacent to a salvage yard in Santa Rosa, one of the few affordable building sites in a one-hundred-mile stretch). "You can't just slap a cross on a building and call it sacred. No, the whole process, start to finish, has to be sacred." You have to go to your roots. Find the well deep within.

That's what they did: start with a sacred piece of ground. You attend to its unique properties; you find the loveliest spot on the acreage and, rather than plop the building on top, you build around it, highlighting, embellishing, adding to. But before that, you listen to the client, the hopes and longings, the call and conviction; you draw that out, what spoke to you and moved you, and then you begin to design.

So that morning we gathered for breakfast at a quiet table in a restaurant in Country Club Plaza shopping center. The restaurant would change hands several times before our project was completed. Never mind that, I doubt they glanced at the menu—*just bring me black coffee.* No, their focus was on the eight "representative" folks around the table and their big writing journals as they went around the table with the question, "When you were little, what was your favorite place? A place you went when you were sad? Or happy or just wanted to be alone? A secret place?"

Where did you find water? Renewal? Grace?

Around the table we went, one person after another: "My grandmother lived out in western Kansas, about two hours west of Wichita. I remember spending summers with her, visiting and drinking freshly squeezed lemonade on the front porch after spending all day in the fields, sweaty, hot, playing hide-and-seek with my cousins."

"Was it a screen porch or just open? Did the front porch door make a sound when you opened it? What about the glass of lemonade . . . in an old mason jar?"

So the conversation had gone. Person after person spoke about the old tire swing that stretched across the creek behind their next door neighbor's house or the hidden cave that was really an old sewer tunnel behind the school, a spot long forgotten by the adults. All the while, the architects wrote down every word in their big journals, asking questions, going deeper, and still deeper.

I knew what they were doing, somewhere deep in my spirit; it was a reflection of my native style, too. I got it as soon as they said it: the more specific you are, the more detailed and nuanced, the greater the chance you will capture the essence of the human experience. If you want to speak to "everyone" in a large room—to have folks leave saying, "I don't know how you knew exactly what I needed to hear today"—then your best shot is to draw as close as you can to your particular, unique story. The closer you get to your roots, the more native, authentic, concrete, and in the lived moment you can be, the more likely you'll touch everyone.

> **The closer you are to your roots, the more authentic your leadership.**

That's how Tall Poppies lead and how I try to lead, whether by crafting a sermon or guiding my fledgling congregation through the endless process of defining our mission. It's never been painting with a broad brushstroke or picking up a pre-fab kit at the big-box hardware store. It's been the painstaking process of listening to person after person as they articulate what keeps them up at night and what sets their toes to tapping.

Many people would come to our award-winning building after the long-awaited dedication, and many would ask, "Could they build this same thing outside of Plano?" "Just east of Louisville?"

Absolutely not.

They'd have to start from scratch. There would be no short-circuiting of the painful, expensive, time-consuming process. That was where the sacredness was found.

So it is with leadership. You start with standing back, up on the ladder, on the Kansas prairie, marking the spot where the sun is brightest at noon, three o'clock, and six o'clock. You are trying to see the horizon, the new earth that could emerge, the "big picture," the vision that will carry you through the decades. You squint and try and imagine the people who will come over the years, the woman, firm in her stride, but bent a bit, too, who knows what she longs for in a church home but has all but given up the search. You see her pulling up in the winding parking lot—carefully crafted to minimize the intrusion of concrete—opening the car door and getting out, taking a deep breath as she makes the journey to the sanctuary for the first time. You see the youth, camped out in "shantytowns" to raise awareness, resources, and funds for services for homeless youth. You try to see the wildest, biggest landscape you can envision, and then you go native and small. You go to your own roots; you find your water in the dry places, in the barren . . .

Along the way, there is more desert, but it's a process. The one-year building project takes two years and then some. The half-a-million-dollar budget swells to a million. The conflicts deepen. Sometimes you misjudge the resources; sometimes they just shift. The architects assumed California skills in eco-building in the Midwest. They were too far out ahead. No one around was doing straw-bale buildings on a commercial level. I believed in financial gifts, offered but not secured. And the plan was subject to no small amount of criticism, which I was too impatient to hear and heed fully. It took four and a half years from our initial phone interview with the architects until the sanctuary dedication. The architects had given heart and soul, but by the time our sanctuary was dedicated in June of 1999—almost ten years after we had formed a building committee—a number of church members and leaders were disgruntled.

We were out of money. The architects were out of money; they did not make a speech to a warm, gracious, appreciative community at the building dedication. They were on the west coast—far away from the accolades and applause. Four years later, they were present at the dedication of the second building, but that is a story for another book.

Leaders Can Miss the Signs

Leaders can overestimate the internal and external resources that are available. In their enthusiasm, they may overestimate the buy-in of needed partners and underestimate the resistance they will face. We can misjudge the terrain, drink too long at the same well, until it all but dries up. Sometimes we underestimate our weaknesses and limitations and overestimate our strength. Sometimes leaders trip and fall.

Tall Poppy that I was, I missed the signals at Saint Andrew that at least a dozen people were done with me. If I hadn't seriously misjudged the terrain and the staff climate, perhaps the ministry of the church could have been strengthened at that point instead of what happened: I was cut down, and the church was left with critical wounds and what might now be an enduring pattern for handling conflict in secretive, destructive ways.

Leaders need to honestly understand the challenges *and* the grace available. They have to know where to find the water. But it can be hard to name our tender and weak places, especially when congregations expect something else. A friend drinks too much, and she has for years. It's how she copes with anxiety, the pain of the past, the fear of the future. Everyone adores her, beautiful, graceful, warm. No one wants to name her drinking problem. Her husband, kids, and friends all shake their heads at her antics: *She loves her Merlot!* Name it differently—*she has a drinking problem; she's an alcoholic*—and a different response is needed.

But even when you've named something correctly, you aren't home free. Take the "wall" that marathoners hit around mile twenty, when legs and lungs are done, but six long miles remain. A classic over-trainer, I may have never hit that wall, but I know the feel of it, the bone-deep weariness, in my emotional life. Some walls I just can't seem to get over: being bossy and demanding and a perfectionist. Those are the walls that are too thick for me to get over. Anyone who struggles with an addiction knows the unyielding nature, the unforgiving side of the wall. We are completely powerless to get over it or through it *on our own*. It takes a higher power—God, Spirit, community, whatever you call it—to get up and over.

It was the twentieth of November, to be exact: the date of my hamstring injury. For twenty-five years, I'd been up at the crack of dawn, running. Last year, I averaged sixty-one miles a week. The hamstring injury knocked me out of my tenth marathon, but more than that, it knocked me out of my life. It disrupted my every pattern, from preaching to sleeping. My friend Misty, who has known me since I was three, has told me for years, "You need to stretch, lift weights, at least take a yoga class." She practices what she preaches; she has kept her body strong through the years with a balance of cardio, strength, and stretching.

Stubbornly, I've said, "No, running is how I make sense of the world. It's my prayer time, mental health time, sermon-writing time. I'm a runner, *period*. Besides, I have zero upper-body strength." It went right over my hard head that a woman who wants to stand upright at eighty needs to build some core strength before she gets there; remember, a Tall Poppy requires a mechanism that allows it to stand.

The first ten days after the injury, I tried to get my heart rate up by bouncing on a mattress with a dumbbell in each hand. Finally, I registered for a yoga class. Rather, my teenage daughter registered me. "Really, you can do it." "Maybe so, but I'm not the agile young woman I once was." She rolled her eyes from a mat she had placed far across the room from mine. "It hurts," I mouthed from my corner.

As my hamstring healed, it became slightly less painful. But, at the time, the fluid style of yoga was too challenging. My daughter Eden said, "Try Pilates. I'll go with you." She was right. The focus on stretching and core strength turned out to be a better fit. The point is not my exercise regime, but my life, our life. I'd foolishly prided myself on being inflexible. *Running is the only thing I can do.* I honestly believed that. The injury was enough of a jolt to make me reconsider some of my fundamental beliefs. Am I really too old to change, to grow, to stretch?

Some flexibility would serve me well.

If You Don't Find the Water, Keep Looking

After I was cut down, I revisited the practice of yoga—for the physical, emotional, and spiritual restoration it offers. When we started Peace Church in the downtown Buddhist temple, there was a space for yoga classes. In the past, I've paced before the second and third sermons of the day. It was different to do an hour of yoga before I preach and lead evening worship. Such a practice helps me mark where the water is in my desert; it strengthens my roots and my core; it takes me to a place of grace and peace within. It reminds me that I need to surrender and trust the well within. What reminds you and helps you trust? What keeps you flexible? What markers do you plant?

Barbara Kingsolver's books and essays are more than enlivenment; she is a leader working for systemic change through her words and work. She lived in Tucson for years, which she described as one million people who live on a space station where everything they eat comes from some refrigerated truck. Even their water. Some water comes from the Colorado River, three hundred miles away, in an open canal. The structures that made her life possible weren't life giving, sustainable. She found it impossible to practice a hundred-mile diet, which is to grow as much of her family food as possible and to buy the rest from farms within a hundred-mile radius. So she moved. As she recounted in her book *Animal, Vegetable, Miracle: A Year of Food Life* (New York: HarperCollins, 2007), she took her family and left the Tucson desert for the rich Virginia family farm.

Not everyone can make that move. She had a farm, and she had a skill that could travel with her. Still, sometimes leaving the desert is the most fruitful choice. Leaders learn—sometimes by painful experience—the high cost of misjudging the resources or staying so long the well dries up. They move on to fertile ground, or not. Sometimes you can't leave, and you just have to keep searching for the well, confident in God's abundance and mercy.

Sometimes, thankfully, a friend has a dream that tells you: get out now—it's past time—and cut your losses. So my friend and colleague Heidi Peterson sent me an e-mail one morning; following her rant against my treatment by others, she wrote:

That is my morning reality check for you.

I had a dream last night that I was at your house. Ben was a baby. Somehow I knew, like you know in dreams that Tom was at work. It was a Friday—my day off, and I was sitting at your dining table. It was winter but the sun was shining. Suddenly the whole house was on fire. You jumped up and dialed 911. Then you ran upstairs and came down dragging Eden by the hand (she was much littler than now) and meanwhile I had picked Ben up off the floor where he was playing. You grabbed a handful of fleece jackets (among them the blue KU one you had on Monday) and we ran out the front door and you kept saying, "I have Eden. You have Ben. Eden and Ben are safe. The rest doesn't matter." Standing in the street in front of your house waiting for the fire trucks you just kept saying, "The kids are okay, right? Okay, we got the kids . . ."

When I woke up it was time for me to get out of bed but I had to lie there and breathe a minute before I could move. If that's MY dream, I can't imagine the nightmares you've been having the last couple of months.

Love you. Heidi

It is, too often, a brutal story: the story of our country's justice system, a repeat of the story of Hagar and Ishmael, banished and left, unseen, to die. Nationally, 49 percent of inmates are African American, despite representing only 13 percent of the population. It is a story of systemic oppression. In this wasteland, Cheryl Pilate stands out. You could pick her out of any lineup. She is tall and striking, and her deep-set eyes draw your gaze.

A newspaper reporter turned social worker turned defense attorney, Cheryl has spent her life searching for water for those who thirst. She has seen the story of Hagar and Ishmael repeated a thousand times—intentional acts of betrayal, one person snitching on another, sending someone into the desert of incarceration.

The wilderness stretches on, but not as far as Cheryl's faith, which reaches back to her family roots in the genocide of the Armenians, and it reaches further still: to the One who preached good news to the poor, sight to the blind, liberty to the oppressed. Her faith is her water in the desert: "I cleanse myself in prayer, in singing, in community . . . the crap I see. It's terrible. My faith is my heart, where I am fed, refueled, nourished so I can go back out there and face it."

Leaders Find Muddy Water, Too

Leaders go to their roots and find God's nourishment and sustenance when there is seemingly none to be had, when the body and soul are barren. What you find, though, when you go to your roots, is complicated, tangled, knotted. Leaders may "go there," but many who follow us are not ready for the journey of introspection, followed, as it has to be, by a commitment to grow and change. Sometimes the water we find is muddy—not good enough or needing more work.

If you are honest, when you go to your roots, when you dig deep for water and search the desert places of your soul, what you find is this: our journeys are not simple, straightforward, or forged with childish faith. Few of us would want our every step traced and set in stone. Our lives are a mixture, complex, good and bad, mud and pure water, faithful and not so faithful. It's always been so, maybe moreso for those called as religious leaders.

Take the colorful prophet Elisha. The book of Kings holds seventeen treasures—little stories about Elisha, the prophet who followed Elijah. I identify with him. In the second chapter of Second Kings, he saves the water supply of a community. He is just passing through, and the people complain about the water. It makes everyone sick. So Elisha, the pastor/prophet on call, throws a stick in the water, and it becomes fresh, clean, safe. He moves along—there is always another hospital to visit—and in the very next scene, the boys in the village come out taunting him, "Bald-head, Bald-head." Annoyed, he sends a mother bear to maul them. When honest, strong leaders reach down deep to draw water from the soul, they find nurture; but they are only human, and sometimes hostility and weariness—mud—appears.

A leader's soul can need purification, too.

He was complicated. As it has turned out, painfully, tragically so. Complicated. We all are. Joe Paterno was far more brilliant, successful, magnetic, determined, and loyal than, well, your average ten people added together. A coach with integrity, he appeared to run a clean football program, with unwavering dedication to the "scholar athletes" he touched, consistently ranking at the top of college football teams in games won and diplomas earned. His adoring fans and family expected him to die on the football field. He did, too. But a long and storied career came to a searing end when he was fired by Penn State for his knowledge of an assistant coach's sexual abuse of minors.

My father lives for college football. Paterno's dismissal was right on the heels of my own at my church. Only my father would associate the two dismissals. It took me several months to ask my dad what he thought about the allegations and incidents, what he really thought about Joe Paterno. He responded as I knew he would, "I think he was an amazing man; I've always admired him, always looked up to him as a model. He was like a dad to so many of his players, but, he missed some things he shouldn't have missed, huge things. I admire him, still."

We are complicated people. When we go to our roots, we find some knots and mud and, always, life-giving water. A man of deep faith, Paterno was cut down, and then he received an aggressive cancer diagnosis that took his life in two months. This leader did what he'd always done: he reached deep and found yet more water in his soul, a spring of unfailing love for himself and others. As he told writer Joe Posnanski, who was at work on a biography of Paterno, "In every life, there have to be some shadows. Look at me. My life has been filled with sunshine. A beautiful and caring wife. Five healthy children. I got to do what I love. How many people are that lucky?"

Leaders find water in the desert. They always have.

Take the Exodus. The Hebrews are slaves in Egypt, mired in the mud pits. Then they cry out, and God hears; God takes note. It's not just their pain and suffering that God sees. God sees their gifts, their potential. God notices Moses, and *God names him* as the one who will lead them home.

When Moses says, "who, me?" God does not say, "Oh, Moses, come on, you'll do great. You are so talented, so above average." No, God says, "I will be with you."

It turns out it's not all up to Moses. It's not up to us, either, to get over the wall, past our anger, our control needs, our addictions.

Finding Passage Through

I was looking for a birthday gift for my daughter, Eden, when she was starting middle school, something inspiring. I came out of the store with a gift for myself instead: a paperweight with a quotation from Ralph Waldo Emerson, "Every wall is a door." It must have spoken to me at the time. I put it on my dresser. Now and then, I've noticed it (on the rare day) when I've moved it to dust. But when I came back from a recent trip to the Middle East—the Holy Land, the land of walls, ancient and new—it caught my eye. *Every wall is a door.*

Hmmm . . . could that really be? Is that possible? From the Holy Land to my own life? For a second I saw myself standing in front of the wall, covered with graffiti. Someone had "tagged" the wall with my strengths: energetic, passionate, doggedly determined. And with my weaknesses: anxious, critical, demanding.

How does all that come together to become a wall—a door—to something more? I thought of the people around me—my childhood friends, my colleagues, and my kids. They were holding sledgehammers and power tools. They rolled up their sleeves and said, "This is nothing, Holly. We've cut through concrete thicker than this with a nail file." I thought of those experiences, too, the hairline cracks that have given way, opened up. The projects that have become doorknobs and handles to the other side.

What if the desert is a door, a door to something new and fresh and fertile? It was for me. I swore I'd never start another new church. The dedication, the passion, the energy, the heart, the risk that was required. I wasn't up to it. At age forty-nine, coming straight out of the wilderness, out of a dry, fearsome place with betrayal, anger, and attacks that I could not have dreamed in my wildest nightmare, I was not yet rehydrated or rested. Yet I started a new church with two locations, which was totally different. Peace Christian Church was really started by the hopes and prayers of a team whose passion, support, and loyalty have turned out to be an oasis in the desert. The water table in this congregation is deep, a stream that never dries up. As a nineteenth-century Danish theologian wrote, it is a spring filled up by the unconditional love of God.

A garden of abundance and bounty, the Sunday table is spread; the homey smell of bread fills the suburban sanctuary and the Buddhist temple. The tables in the narthex have sign-up sheets for gleaning days for the hungry. And, on many Sundays, chocolate cake to celebrate. We celebrate everything we can, small and large: a new baby, a baptism, a release from prison, anything, honestly, we can celebrate. We know that God is good, all the time, and all the time, God is good.

There is much to celebrate, always. Thanks be to God for the desert places.

chapter four
Leaders Part the Waters of Conflict and Discontent

It was one of those "driveway moments" they speak about on public radio. As I was leaving for work, I heard an essay in the "This I Believe" series. From Colin Powell to a waitress at a diner, thousands of people submit personal and colorful story-essays that speak to their core values. This one was from a columnist with the *San Francisco Chronicle*, Jon Carroll. My ears perked up because I think of the challenge facing the columnist and the preacher as somewhat parallel: both constantly have to come up with new material.

Carroll opened his essay with his words of advice to his granddaughter on her first day of kindergarten:

> I wished her success. Later I thought, I should have wished her failure. Success is boring. Success is proving you can do something you already know you can do. Failure is how we learn. . . . I earn my living by writing a daily newspaper column. Each week I am aware that one

column is going to be the worst column of the week. I don't set out to write it; I try my best every day. Still, every week, one column is inferior to the others. Sometimes spectacularly so. . . .

I have learned to cherish that column [the worst column in the week's series]. A successful column usually means I'm treading on familiar ground, going with the tricks that work, preaching to the choir. Often in my inferior columns, I am trying to pull off something that I've never done before. Something I'm not sure can be done. (Jon Carroll, "Failure Is a Good Thing," This I Believe, NPR [Oct. 9, 2006], www.npr.org/templates/story/story.php?storyId=6196795)

Leaders, Even Good Ones, Don't Always Get It Right

There is an inevitability to failure, especially if you are the one to put your spade in first. Sometimes you strike pay dirt, and sometimes you strike rock. Leaders fail, sometimes painfully. From attorneys to politicians to pastors: leaders understand that *every wall is also a door*. The impasse is just temporary and represents an opportunity to grow and to stretch. The pastor who designed a sabbatical around intentional engagement in Israeli-Palestinian conflict understood that moving forward meant using conflict to find a way beyond the impasse.

Consider a colleague of mine who received a great deal of criticism for her leadership during a controversy around holy unions in her congregation. In the end, she'd "won" and been able to perform the ceremony. But a few members left the church as a result. She responded, "What really hurt was that I knew there is a kernel of truth in their criticisms of me and my failings." There always is. Leaders find a way to take the nuggets of truth and make gold out of them.

As Bernie Lyon and Dan Moseley say, we will not always get it right:

> Sometimes it is only by getting it wrong (dramatically so), that we come to know better what might be creatively possible. We can only know the consequences of the strategies we develop after we have acted. Leading congregations in conflict, then, is trying, failing, forgiving, and learning from our efforts and allowing those to shape our next efforts. (*How to Lead in Church Conflict: Healing Ungrieved Loss* [Nashville: Abingdon, 2012], p. 9)

Or, as the magnet on my refrigerator proclaims: "Unless you are attempting something you have not yet mastered, you will never grow."

Still, nothing is more painful than being cut down and having to take root, again, in the compost left behind. So they are taking some swipes at you? Good. It means you are a leader. People take shots at leaders. They try and take them down. People are funny that way, especially with pastors. Some in the congregation will set you on a pedestal only so they can knock you off. But your response is up to you. You can use this to grow. But you've got to ask yourself the tough questions: how did I miss this? How did I not see this coming?

It is hard to reflect on the tough questions, especially if you've failed big time. But the message is clear and repeated by one wise person after another: "This is a good thing; it will make you a better leader"; "It sounds like this really hit a nerve; that's a blessing." Losing the church I founded and served for twenty-one years didn't feel like it was a good thing, a blessing, a learning opportunity. It felt like the end of my life as I knew it. And for me, it was the end of my life as I had known it. To say that I was lost and anxious doesn't come close to describing the toll that being cut down took on me. A pastor, a Tall Poppy, doesn't come back overnight after being cut down. The recovery period is long—one step forward and a hundred steps back—and fraught with unimaginable stresses and challenges. For me, that period of acute anxiety lasted for over a year.

I was at the "top of my game." Really. Literally, I was at the pinnacle of my career. I was the opening preacher at our denomination's biannual general gathering. Three days later, I sat down for lunch with Abingdon Press editor Kathryn Armistead. She offered an invitation for conversation about a book—this book, a book I had never thought about writing—on leadership. Less than confident, I jumped in. I knew instantly it was a page-turning, life-changing opportunity. Just the kind of situation I crave—working with an exceptionally bright woman who is a few years ahead of me on the journey. Little did I know what would happen next. Six days later, I had the book and a few sequels outlined and pulled together, so I thought. On the seventh day, I received an e-mail five minutes after my plane landed for what was supposed to be a delightful thirty-six-hour vacation. All I was told was that there was an urgent personnel matter that needed my attention. And on the seventh day, my song began.

Being Cut and Left for Dead

Shock. That's the only word I have to describe what happened next: a meeting was called. I was confronted with a letter demanding my resignation within three days. My understanding is that this was a secret kept from the board and the congregation. I refused to bend. The cut came after the dust settled and I was still standing. After twenty-one years of pastoring one of our denomination's leading congregations—in numbers, mission, worship, education—I was cut to the core and trampled.

> What people may mean for evil, God means for good.

I had been a Tall Poppy in my denomination and in my community. I had no idea what was next or even what to do next. I couldn't see past tomorrow. I had lost the vision. I was in total shock. What kind of leader was I really?

I wrote these words two days before I was called home and, with no warning, asked to resign:

I'm writing this book to share a few things I've figured out in twenty-five years in ministry—most of it, twenty-one years now, in the congregation I still serve as the founding pastor. I've found a way of leading that is enlivening and empowering for the people I serve—but, perhaps more importantly, a way of leading that leaves me, most days, energetic and eager for the next day with its challenges. And most days, I'm having a good time. The congregation is flourishing. I'm healthier than ever and living out of my best and truest self.

I offer these reflections, not as an exhaustive work on leadership, but as pearls that have come to me at some significant price. If you can avoid the stress and distress I've felt and get "there" quicker, I'll be the first to say amen.

That shows how clueless I was, overestimating commitment and misjudging my environment. Where did I go wrong? I was a Tall Poppy, after all! At the time I did not fully appreciate the fact that leadership is a double-edged sword. This experience spoke to a side of leadership that I had never fully considered. As I gain distance, I see that some people set the pastor on a pedestal—seeming to be closer to God—and some knock the pastor off. Still, perhaps I was perceived as indifferent or insensitive. Because I was the founding pastor, this church was almost like my child, and I can also see that it was hurting, having been traumatized as well. This thought, almost more than anything else, hit the most tender places in my heart.

In their insightful and hopeful work *How to Lead in Church Conflict: Healing Ungrieved Loss,* Lyon and Moseley describe unresolved grief as the heart of conflict:

> the failure to grieve early life losses well often produces . . . conflict between persons in groups: Individuals defend themselves against the emotional pain of their ungrieved losses in ways that conflict with one another, that do not allow them to see the real other interacting with them. (p. 52)

The leader's ability to grieve "well" is central as attack and loss are inevitable for pastors, particularly bold, courageous pastors and leaders. Leadership requires an understanding of the complex, unconscious nature of conflict. Leaders are not ones who "know what to do" but those who can "grieve well." They are so right on the challenge of grieving, especially when loss occurs so suddenly and so painfully.

Theologian Serene Jones describes the experience and process of trauma as something that happens not just to those who directly experience violence. She says our minds are like offices and store incoming information and stimuli in one of the thousands of files we have created to make sense of our world. When trauma occurs, the incoming information is so overwhelming we have no idea where to store it. It fits none of our categories, and we are stunned. Over time we usually do make sense of what happened and respond, hopefully in creative ways.

"Diabolical!" my friend Cheryl said after the details of the plot to take me down came to light. Diabolical. She repeated it. The chief of medicine at a hospital, a preacher's kid, and a mom, she had seen how people can act up and act out in a community, even one designed to heal: "Diabolical! It is unbelievable how people can band together to destroy. How there can be such vengeance, such a desire to destroy the other? You've come right up to the edge of the darkness and seen it. That's overwhelming."

As leaders, pastors see the very best people can be, but also we see the very worst. We see goodness and light in some faces but darkness and fear in others. We see how when people feel vulnerable, darkness can block out the light. Evil doesn't win in the end, but in the short run it can put up a good contest. You hear it in the Scriptures. Our fore-parents in the faith weren't naive. Mixed in with words of praise are words of anxiety, even fear, about what lurks beneath the surface. Psalm 139 speaks of Leviathan—the sea creature—a monster, but also an acknowledgment that what is beyond our vision and beneath our subconscious can be ugly, harrowing, destructive.

After the big blowup, Misty and I were driving past an intersection that had a portable shredding machine parked on it. The sign in front read: "Shredding Event this Saturday." I thought about our church. A shredding event. That is what it had been put through. My friend Misty pointed out the window. It didn't do just to throw something (or someone) out; people have to shred it.

Much more difficult than the shock and disorientation is the grief, like the grief of a mother suffering the loss of a child. As events unfolded, I felt like I was lost at sea. I sat at the table in my office and tried to comprehend what they were saying, like I was in the emergency room with my son, Ben, after an accident and the doctor was telling me he wasn't going to make it. I was doubled over, arms folded tightly across my stomach, my body shaking. In the previous week, I'd feasted with visitors and new members at that table, listened to a newly engaged couple, and made marketing plans for the fall. This was unbelievable. It couldn't be happening. I literally thought I would die. In the six months that followed, the amount of grief to process was crushing. I thought of what a friend sent me after her child died, unexpectedly:

> There is just so much to grieve. There are the broken places I knew but now feel in a deeper way. My core loss/grief: my mother was (and is) unable to soothe me. She is a lovely person; she appears calm and quiet. But, her spirit races with anxiety. Small problems are magnified. At the heart of every narrative there is a fear of total destruction. When I was three, my father died; when I was nine, my mother was in a car wreck and nearly died. For the next year,

I had to help care for her. I feel like I've spent my lifetime trying to keep her alive. When my own son died, my first thought was, "I cannot let my mother know. It would destroy her."

Grief: The Head Waters of Discontent

Grief takes its toll on our spirits and our ministries. It can put us adrift. I never experienced depression until the loss of my ministry. I found myself bouncing back and forth between anxiety and, worse, the overwhelming feeling of being tired. I'd honestly give anything never to feel that way again. The loss of so many relationships, hundreds and hundreds, was monumental. It was the death of a dream and the death of twenty-one years of my life. There was no way to separate my life from what I'd spent more than two decades creating. My entire home (and basement) was filled with the church—true, particularly, for anyone who has gone thirteen years without a real office and has worked from home.

Grieving is difficult work. It is nothing more or less than giving birth. I think of a woman I knew in my first call who was pregnant with her first child. She and her husband had tried to conceive for three years. The news of their pregnancy was greeted with delight from friends and family coast to coast. At nineteen weeks, the doctor found a tumor. He thought the baby could survive it; but at twenty-five weeks, the tumor won, and the baby died. Barbara had two choices: having a Ceasarean section or delivering the baby while awake. She chose to give birth to death.

That is the work of grief. It is labor. It is the most difficult work we ever do. It is allowing our bodies and our souls to feel the deep loss we have known. I appreciate the Jewish tradition of shiva after the death of a loved one. For seven days, traditionally, the family "sit shiva" and mourn the death. The holy number seven hearkens back to the creation taking place over seven days. If it takes seven days to create the world, it takes at least seven days to mourn its destruction. During that time, family members are to be relieved of other responsibilities so they can mourn. Friends bring food, clean, and attend to details.

> **Leaders need to cultivate friends and mentors for the tough times.**

The practice of sitting shiva, or, as in the ancient Middle East, paying professional mourners, underscores the truth: grieving takes work, attention, and focus. Walter Brueggemann speaks about the centrality of grieving in his work on the prophets. Two things are central to the movement of faith: grieving and amazement. The prophet/pastor/priest must, as Moses did, enable the people to cry out, to grieve, and to criticize before they can move on to hope, vision, and the future.

Leaders who have not grieved their own conflicts, their own disappointments, cannot separate the waters of discontent; they cannot confront the sea monsters. The challenge is large: leaders have not only their own grief to process during conflict but also the grief of their parishioners—a grief that, when left unresolved, comes out in destructive ways.

That is easier said than done. As Lyon and Moseley suggest,

> Some people will hide, others will come at you, some will be forceful, and others will be quiet; some will bite down and hold on, while others will try to appease; some will recruit supporters, and some will feel lost and alone. Some will try to do your job for and better than you and some will not do even their own job at all. Getting askew is a complex thing. (pp. 47–48)

Leaders must have foresight and maintain a non-anxious presence especially in the midst of conflict. If you need help doing that or are too close to the situation, you must call in reinforcements and get support for yourself. But we must also be aware that because we stand out, there are always others who want our role; they may not want to be us, but they sometimes want what they *perceive* we have—power and control or perhaps simply recognition and the positive esteem of others. As we face the waters of discontent as leaders, we must not forget the irrational forces of group life, even in the church, that push and pull us all in powerful ways. Yet, the key is to accept correction with grace and to continue to offer God's love.

Learn to be that non-anxious presence.

We will not always get it right. I certainly did not. Sometimes it is only by getting it wrong that we come to know better what might be creatively possible. As Bernie Lyon and Dan Moseley would say, I had stepped out of my role. Leaders become "askew" during the conflict; they do not always *take* the role of leader but are at times *taken* by the role. But these moments, when you are lost, also offer the deepest possibilities for growth. Too many times I had failed to acknowledge that conflict is not a sidebar of leadership but is central to it. Regrettably, the liquid, chaotic times we live in produce ever more intense and protracted conflicts. Leaders who stand tall will receive the brunt of attacks from those whom they seek to lead.

Parting Waters Can Mean Parting Ways

Tall Poppy leaders understand that growth requires change and that change brings loss—and, by nature, conflict. Congregations are caught between wanting growth, even spiritual growth, and wanting stability. Leading in such an environment takes the capacity to "mentalize"—to engage the conflict thoughtfully and wisely. To lead effectively requires an honest acknowledgment of the scene, setting, and conflict that are always present.

Like many leaders, I've been able to push forward, in spite of others at times, because of my belief in my own strength and talent. That said, even the strongest have their limits. A critical part of leadership is seeing those limits and liabilities honestly and addressing them effectively.

I haven't always been there.

The blood on my light green running shirt is a testament to that. Running is how I organize and make sense of my life. I run every morning, almost without exception, in temperatures of eight below or 106 degrees. I run. Pounding the pavement is where my preaching happens, my reflection, my prayer. I read the scripture, listen to public radio, and then head out to start organizing my weekly sermon. Running helps me keep my feet planted on the ground. Sunday is the last important run: getting the sermon "in my head." My Sunday run is usually a six- or seven-mile run around 5:30 a.m. But not this one Sunday, three years ago. It was early fall, maybe September or October. It was still pitch dark, so I was running in our neighborhood. I saw something swoop down several times—a hawk or a bat. I noticed but didn't think much of it until running back down the street I felt something hit my head—hard. It took a good minute or more for me to realize my head was bleeding, badly. I felt something warm and wet going down my back. An hour later, I was at church and preached all three services. I tell this story because it makes the point: it takes a lot to knock me down. That's not always good, because to lead and keep the vision out in front, leaders have to keep an honest look at the terrain and the conflicts that are present.

Finding Healing in Living Water

No matter how good our leadership is, sometimes we just mess up. We just screw up. We just don't get it right. But what distinguishes Tall Poppy leaders is that they are able to draw on the Source for their strength. In John 4, Jesus asks a woman if she would like "living water." It surely struck her as an odd question because what she heard was, "Do you want deep well water?" "Living water" and "deep well water" are the same in Aramaic. And obviously because no one has living water, he surely must mean deep well water. But as readers of the New Testament, we know otherwise. When things get tough, we look for connections to the Source of Living Water, but we also look for connection to significant, trusted relationships that can buffer blows and help keep events in perspective.

Healing is a process that can be helped along by friends who "sit shiva" with us. That's one central way for leaders to find healing: to accept grace and care from friends, family, and companions who offer acceptance and unconditional love. The night after I was confronted in my office, Carla came over with a pesto quiche and dark chocolate cookies. Heidi, busy with her own church and family, went to meetings on my behalf, came over to my house, helped me cook for my family, and listened to me for hours at a time—each day. Others took my children for coffee or to a baseball game or had them spend the night. Cindy sent cards, my parents drove up for a visit, Cheryl and Michael sent chocolate, Misty met me in Tulsa for a weekend of planning, and Kris and Liz sent strategy ideas. Lee convinced me I was strong enough to write about it, that the Tall Poppy can, in fact, defy gravity. The hundreds of cards I received in the mail, along with pressed flower petals, are in a box on the top shelf in my closet. As I look back, all I can honestly say is, "That's how I got through it."

That's the heart of the story of Rebekah and Isaac, the thirst for healing in a world where the water dries up or, perhaps worse, is churned up and muddied. Their story begins with the near sacrifice of Isaac. Abraham had him all tied up, was about to do him in, when God provided the ram. In the Midrash, Isaac is often portrayed as wounded, broken, and grieving from this deep emotional wound. The rabbis said Isaac suffered a kind of death when his father almost sacrificed him, a primal loss. So, they asked, how did he get beyond this intense emotional wounding? Rebekah.

Rebekah was beautiful, and she was a virgin, which was important in the ancient world, for it was a signal that she would not bring shame upon the family and that she could be controlled. But there is more to this story than initially meets the eye; and it represents a step forward for women because Rebekah wore the pants in her family. The relationship between husband and wife was about mutuality, companionship, the stretching of roles. Compared to Isaac, she is the proactive one, defined by active verbs. In meeting Abraham's servant at the well, she runs, she draws water, she fills jars, then she fills more jars, and then she fills even more jars. Hospitable, too, like Abraham who ran to meet the visiting angels and hurried to feed them, Rebekah ran to the camels and to the well, and she hurried to lower her jar and empty it again and again. Some early stories assume that Rebekah was the only person who didn't know that Isaac's father nearly killed him, but somehow she saw the comfort and care that he needed. It was love that brought healing. If Abraham had wives and Jacob had cowives, Isaac and Rebekah are the first romantic love story in Scripture. By her sensitive love, he was healed because she knew what he needed before he could even speak it.

After the confrontation in my office in which I was asked to resign, hundreds of people stepped up to support me—more attorneys than you can count, dear friends, church members, my parents, and even my children. Two of the most powerful words came from my kids. On a day I was to speak before the congregation, Eden, seventeen at the time, came up and put a necklace with an owl charm (remembering how I was attacked by what turned out to be an owl, but stood back up, bloody head and all). After three months of turmoil, my thirteen-year-old son, Ben, looked up at me from the breakfast table and, said, "Mom, you need to quit saying you are sorry. You have said that enough for a lifetime."

Parting Your Own Seas of Discontent

Leaders part the seas of discontent by beginning with their own. They commit to the long journey toward healing, and they put processes in place that will address conflict and, eventually, bring healing, which finally brings us to forgiveness.

When we began Peace Christian Church, we were intentional about naming the loss we all brought to this new setting. We had to be. Literature on churches that start out of conflict say that such churches are prone to more conflict and that ungrieved losses can manifest themselves in yet more conflict. The downside of starting out fresh and making new choices is that not everyone will agree with every choice. That's part of any new venture. People play a role in your life but sometimes that role ends. For the most part, the people attracted to Peace were nimble, open, flexible, the kind of folks who can adjust well to the changes, recognizing that compromises are essential to the health of any group.

Our pastoral partners—the lay persons who are in the ministry of support and care—designed healing sessions with a psychologist who had practice in working with grief in a group setting. We addressed loss and hope in worship through careful selection of scripture and song. We put in place teams in which people could be of service and also could find ways to connect with one another. The structure committee spent hundreds of hours, collectively, on the bylaws and on the decision to nest in a Buddhist temple and a traditional suburban church. We operate in an atmosphere for which we have created structures in which we can hear divergent views. When we chose Ruth to direct our programs and administration, we were keenly aware of the match in temperament, skill, passion, loyalty, and faith that is necessary in a strong, balanced working relationship between a high-energy pastor and her staff.

The constructive use of conflict is a function of leadership. After all, parting the waters isn't the point, but crossing into something new is. Conflict is not about an occasional flare-up but is a part of every organization. Like that of a couple, the relationship between a leader and a community involves stretching, reaching the goal at times, and falling short at others. And starting over. For the cycle to be healthy, the leader has to practice grieving, healing, *and* forgiving.

Crossing into Forgiveness

I wanted to see the ocean. California locals didn't understand because they see it all the time, or maybe, living this close, they never see it. I had asked several folks, "which way to the ocean," and they had hesitated, as though they hadn't thought about the calm, refreshing, restorative water in a long time. To me, coming from Kansas and the churn and challenge of caring for children and a church, this three-day speaking engagement had been worth it for the chance to see the ocean.

The first day had been a bust. Trapped with a friend in Southern California traffic, I was three hours late and I missed the chance to see the ocean. I woke up the second morning determined to see it. The bellman said, "To run there and back will take a couple of hours." I had run a marathon earlier in the month, so I set out running. I could see it, not far into the run, but I hadn't counted on the gated communities, the cliffs, and the lanes of traffic to cross. But I was determined to see the water, soothing, satisfying, immense.

Running along, my mind went to a friend from seminary I'd seen at the event. We had been close in school but were now separated by miles; we had seen little of each other since graduation. A committed pastor and a gifted preacher, Jennifer was fired after just a year at her most recent church. Tall, spirited, independent, an outspoken leader in her community, she was also sensitive and attentive to the needs of her parishioners. She was bruised. You could see it in her face. I asked her what went wrong: "I'm not sure," she shook her head. "There were factions, a history of conflict, and I got caught in the middle. I don't know what happened, it's still too close, too fresh." She's right; it's hard to understand a conflict when you can't even breathe. When you hold your womb because the fear of loss is so core; when you are askew, disoriented; when your words, thoughts, and mind are racing; when your life—financially, emotionally, spiritually—has been upended, sleep won't come.

Take, for example, one of the original Tall Poppy leaders, the Apostle Paul. He had friction with the church at Corinth. Now, it's impossible for the wisest scholars to piece it back together. He'd started the church, loved them dearly, worked beside them spreading the word, and then gone on to another ministry. Somehow the waters of discontent were stirred. Some questioned Paul's integrity. He'd said he would come for a visit and didn't. Some said he was wishy-washy, with his yes not a yes, and his no not a no. Whatever the problem, Paul was hurt, defensive: *Look at me. Look at all I've done for you.* He was sure it was just a misunderstanding. He would rush over there, make a quick call, get it cleared up.

You've been there. You've had a problem and thought you could just quickly clear it up, only to have every attempt to fix it only make it worse. Paul's second trip to Corinth was a disaster. He got into some kind of ruckus; someone offended him deeply, called him a name, insulted him publicly. We're not sure, but he was furious and it showed. He left in a huff and fired off the kind of letter that the therapist tells you never to send. You know the kind: just jot it all down on paper and let it all out, but make sure no one else sees it. The helpful spouse might see it lying on the desk and mistakenly put it in the mailbox. Or, in a fit of anger, still hot, you might type out your thoughts and hit the send button.

Paul regretted it later. Truly. He said so in the seventh chapter. He wished he'd never written that. In the end, though, it turned out OK. Paul went on to write from a place of reconciliation and healing. But how they got to healing, just like how they got cross-wise initially, has been lost. No doubt Paul would say it came the way forgiveness always comes: as grace, as a gift, as an ocean of mercy and forgiveness washing over us. Paul would speak, inevitably, of healing. *Anyone in Christ is a new creation. The past is finished and gone. Everything is fresh and new. We who have been buried with Christ have been raised with him. Nothing can separate us from the love of Christ.*

But there is more here, something that Paul did. It's a move that is instructive and ultimately redemptive. It's a move that can instruct us when we find ourselves in sight of the turbulent seas but are unable to get to the calm of the healing water. Paul makes this move—we've seen him do it before—from *I* to *we*. It quits being about how he's been hurt and becomes about what is replenishing and restorative for the community. He says, if anyone has caused pain, he has caused it not to me but, to some extent, to all of you.

Take my friend, Jennifer, who was fired from her church; her concern was for the community. "Folks are so hurt," she said. The sadness she felt was not solely for herself, but for those around her who had missed a chance to make peace, to live out the gospel. Paul got there, but sometimes we can't.

I finally got to the ocean, only to find a cliff. To run down the path and back up would have made me late for a luncheon at which I was to give the opening prayer. Discouraged I had missed the chance to stick my toes in the water, I headed back to the hotel and then saw something I had completely missed on the way to the ocean: a landmark that was worth a ten-mile run and a flight to California—the Salk Institute.

Six months earlier, I would have run right past the massive stone building that was sitting back from the road and was rhythmically framing and responding to the ocean. It would have meant nothing to me, save the recent film about Louis Kahn, a leading architect of the twentieth century. The institute, like the capitol building of Bangladesh and the libraries at Yale University, was his gift to the world.

The film was not really about Louis Kahn or his work, but about his son, Nathaniel. When Kahn died, he left behind groundbreaking buildings and something else: two wives and two families—one family whom the world knew about and one who was hidden, that he went visited only by cover of night. That hidden family was not mentioned when he died in 1974. Kahn's obituary was on the cover of *The New York Times*, but Nathaniel, eleven years of age at the time, and his sister and mother were not mentioned. They were unclaimed and unacknowledged. Thirty years later, Nathaniel went on a journey to "find" his father, to make peace with him. It was a journey of forgiveness and reconciliation, a journey that took him from New England to the west coast and halfway around the world to the impoverished country of Bangladesh, where his father had designed and built a capitol, breathtaking and soul-lifting, for the poorest of the poor.

Nathaniel's journey was the journey of everyone who seeks to lead and to follow the forgiving love of God. There is more to his story and to ours. Louis Kahn was more than one thing. Like all of us, he was complicated. An inadequate father, he was also a genius who created spaces that brought majesty from the human spirit. At one point in the film, Nathaniel goes to see the capitol building in Bangladesh. The young man we meet in the film is not bitter, but we can imagine him looking at the building and then looking away. We see what a child feels when he is invisible and overlooked by a parent. But in Bangladesh, people just fell over him, telling him how much they loved his father, how generous he had been to create a masterpiece for them. The guide says, "Maybe he wasn't such a great dad, but he is our hero." By widening the lens of his father beyond his own experience,

Nathaniel finds healing, a window to see his father. Nathaniel can cross through the waters of discontent to see a more complete picture of a father who had something deeply wrong inside but also something deeply right.

The closing scene is mystically gorgeous, cinematically and theologically. Nathaniel is roller-blading on the plaza of the Salk Institute. The camera enhances the scene, speeds it up, plays with it as the son skates around and around, up and over the sides of the building, the blue of the ocean and sky stretching on forever behind him.

Light, ocean, sky, a mature man who is playful, joyful, peaceful. We see a scene of reconciliation, the waters of discontent calmed. The scene is intensely private and yet very public, inviting us in.

> ### Leaders need to forgive those who won't or can't be led.

In my life, forgiveness has come quickly, much of the time. Yet, there have been moments in which healing has felt elusive, like the ocean's edge. I can see it but somehow cannot find my way down the path. Leaders come out of each conflict wiser, stronger, with new skills and sensitivities. But leaders are complicated. We are a mixture of good and bad, successes and failures. Particularly in such moments, we need Rebekahs in our life who provide unconditional love; we need a community that prays for us; and we need scriptures and stories that instruct and guide us toward a deeper connection to the healing power of God.

My friend Lee sent some questions to help me journal during this difficult time. Here is one question that was especially helpful. Perhaps it will also be meaningful to you. *How do you keep your face turned toward the sun when the shadows and cloud cover threaten to take away your light?* I wrote:

I love to sit in the sunshine.

I spent the year in the windowsill when I was a senior in Mrs. Basham's Honors English. That's who I am. I always move toward the light. There is something in the feeling of sunshine on my skin that brings the grace of God so close to me.

Not just sunshine, worship, too.

It was now the second day of my leave of absence. My mood was a roller coaster—up one minute and then down the next. I'd had lunch with a trusted colleague. We had been working for the better part of a year on plans for collaboration between our congregations. Both churches have a deep heart for worship, care, and mission. My colleague had served his congregation for a dozen years or so. It had been a rich ministry, but the last five years had been ones of struggle. When we began exploring collaboration, his congregation had exhausted several options for financial viability. Our churches had forged a plan we felt was rich with possibility and hope. Then I was cut down. It threatened my ministry and ended, just as it had been announced, the possibility for collaboration. It was sobering to see my colleague's disappointment. Still, seeing him gave me hope. When you work collaboratively with people you treasure and trust you do your best work. Maybe great things can still happen.

> **It always comes down to God's unconditional love.**

Something in his faithful spirit said resurrection and . . . worship. That's what keeps my face turned toward the light. Worship is healing and restorative in every way.

What keeps your face turned toward the light? Is it the presence of God in it all and through it all? Worship. Being present. What else keeps me turned toward the light? Prayer. Family. Friends. For me, running. What is it for you? That's where we start and end: in the promise, the promise of God's presence, of the resurrection, of the new heaven and the new earth, the promise that there is yet more up ahead. A new vision beckons.

chapter five

Leaders Weed and Prune

She was all of thirty-four years old, with three kids under six years, when she was diagnosed with uterine cancer. Her doctor shook her head at the scan and looked back at the charts. "Did you miss a yearly appointment? Maybe we were so busy delivering the girls we missed something." By that time it had spread. It was hard to understand how her womb could shelter the babies with the cute dark curls and also shelter this growth, a bundle of cancer cells that would choke off her life. How? Why? It's what we always ask.

Sorting the Good, Bad, and Ugly

The good mixed with the bad. The life-giving mixed with the deadly. There is the parable that only the Gospel writer Matthew tells. In this parable, there are two sowings and two types of seeds: good and bad, wheat and weeds. In the first sowing, the farmer scatters the good seed. At night, an enemy comes and scatters the bad. When the wheat sprouts, the weeds do, too. The slaves go to the owner and say, "How did that happen? Didn't you sow good seed?" And the householder says, "Yes, but the enemy came during the night and sowed this bad seed." The servants ask, "Should we pull it up?" "No, or you might get some of the wheat. Wait until the harvest. Collect the weeds and burn them; gather the wheat into my barn."

Unlike the oft-repeated Parable of the Sower, in which growth depends on where the seeds land, this story is more problematic, and separating the wheat from the weeds is painstaking, time-consuming, and done by hand. Pull indiscriminately and you risk killing everything and never have bread. But more, the parable points to a truth we don't like to see: there are healthy and not-so-healthy elements in every field and in every person. Life is complicated, and so are congregations. You cannot divide the world, neatly, into the guys in dark hats and guys in white hats.

I remember seeing the movie *The Bad Seed* as a little girl. It was about another little girl, with a sweet smile, frilly dress, and blond braids who is wicked to the core. She commits murder; she is a bad seed. Much as we might want to separate people into categories of good and evil, in truth, brokenness, anger, selfishness, and the ability to hurt and wound are a part of all of us. An American soldier kills a dozen civilians in Afghanistan. He is paid by us, hired by us, trained by us, and sent far away to do what we can't seem to say no to. He is "us."

I remember the day the Vietnam War came home to my corner house in Arlington, Texas. I played, day in and day out, with the boys in the other corner houses—cowboys against the Indians, Germans against the Americans. But there was another war raging. A brother of one of the mothers in a corner house had returned from Vietnam and had started a helicopter company. One night he took a gun and killed his wife and four children before turning the gun on himself. Bad seeds were sown at night. In some scriptures, the nighttime symbolizes sloth, a time when our defenses are down, when evil can enter in, when the enemy comes. In this parable, though, night is natural, a time for sleep, for rest. Anger, aggression, and even rage are not foreign species that have invaded but are part of our human condition.

The young mother lay on the hospital bed. Her young children had just left after a short visit, perhaps the last visit. As a young pastor, I remember thinking, how could this tumor have grown in her womb, where only life should grow? She had smiled weakly, touched her womb, and looked up at me: sometimes the good grows along with the bad. If the tumor had been discovered earlier, the girls wouldn't be here.

> Simple, easy answers don't work, but love will prevail.

The parable promises that all will be sorted out at the harvest, in God's good time, with compassion and mercy. In the meantime, leaders work in the light of day, to till and keep the gardens that are in our care, to separate, thoughtfully, the healthy from the not-so-healthy, providing an environment in which that which is abundant and sustaining can bear fruit. When we look the other way, for whatever reason—because we are fatigued, distracted, averse to conflict, or just plain oblivious—then the negative, unhealthy elements can take root. Bad seeds produce and reproduce, and we have the next conflict in the bedroom, boardroom, or war room.

Weeding and Pruning Are Constant Tasks of Leadership

It was a time of delightful productivity for me. It was summertime; my husband and son were out west for six weeks. With a quiet house, I was hard at work on a book proposal and a sermon for General Assembly. I followed the same daily routine: rising early, reading, running, working through ideas on my run, writing, then getting down to the daily work of e-mail, pastoral care, and programming. Meanwhile, people were at work on a plan to end my ministry, a plan begun months earlier, without the knowledge of the congregation or leadership. I have to take responsibility: I neglected the important work of Tall Poppy leadership—the work of weeding and pruning. Ignoring this step, failing to attend to the tangible presence of tension, disagreement, and anxiety, led to the escalation of friction and the eruption of conflict.

It eventually cost me my position. Leaders have to weed and prune continuously. I didn't. I'm not entirely sure why.

In part, I was more interested in planting new seeds than in looking at areas in the church that had grown toxic or dormant. Some of it was classical conflict-avoidant behavior; situations involving confrontation are not my favorite. Supervision and evaluation, when the situation is difficult, require muscles and techniques I have not fully developed. I prefer running and yoga to digging up dandelions or pruning my rosebushes; I hate to see that which has been beautiful be cut and fall to the ground. Conflict is most difficult to address when the relationships involved are old, even overgrown, when the personalities are tender, even prickly—a composition of love and resentment, appreciation and envy, joy and annoyance.

Weeding and Pruning Are Done in the Light

There were signals, though, that a section of the garden was growing out of control. In late winter, I felt an increased tension and resistance with a few members of the church. That spring, I focused my time working with a mentor on increasing both cohesion and communication among staff. Still, in my gut, I remember thinking something was up. The day after the demand for my resignation, I thought back to mid-May. I remember being puzzled and oddly concerned when the window for spring planting came and went and the usual gifts of seedlings from a church member did not come. Then there were other exchanges. It seemed to me that not everything was being done in the light, but I was in the dark, too, and couldn't see it. I only had a disquieting feeling.

June offered a climate for the perfect storm. I was off the continent for the first week, which provided ideal conditions for the plan to be firmed and finalized. Added to that, I rarely worked in my office at the church. For the first thirteen years, when there were no offices, I had become accustomed to working from my kitchen table, a practice I returned to when the kids were teenagers. Meanwhile, I wasn't giving enough thought to all that I should have. I wasn't fulfilling my role as leader fully. As Lyon and Moseley point out, a "boundary violation can also involve a failure to perform one's role fully, a stepping too far back from the boundary of the role we have in the congregation—not doing too much, but too little" (pp. 66–67).

We walk in the light as he is in the light.

After I was cut down, my mentor, Susan, pointed out that a leader is at increased risk when she gets the "big stage." The demand for my resignation was on the closing day of our denomination's General Assembly, for which I was the opening preacher—far and away, the biggest honor of my career. Missing the signals was a monumental lapse. What took twenty-one years to build was cut down in six days.

Our souls, communities, and country exist in fields with both wheat and weeds. Life and leadership entail risk, so we minimize our vulnerability to attack by carefully, consistently attending to the tangled and the toxic. Leaders understand a dynamic organization requires a proactive, fluid approach to ministry resources, staffing, and mission. Leaders constantly prune the short-term challenges for the long-term vibrancy of the mission.

Fruitfulness Depends on Weeding and Pruning

I can't pass up a dark chocolate mousse, but fig cookies are no temptation for me. Figs are a delicacy, though, in the Middle East, where you can buy them in gold-wrapped boxes, served candied and sweet or freshly peeled at dinner.

In Jesus' day, figs were a symbol of blessing, peace, and prosperity. So Jesus' harsh words against the barren fig tree during Passover were hard to figure. Fig trees weren't supposed to be in season—it was a good six weeks before the June harvest. What seems more out of season is Jesus' response, unless we also understand that the fig tree was a symbol of God's people. As uncomfortable as this story may make us, it points to Jesus' concern that we bear fruit. Pruning is necessary if the long-term goal is faithfulness. But pruning is never meant to be the end of the story. Mercy and hope are the true fruit of the harvest. Jesus' mission was not defoliating and destroying. The point of pruning is the restoration of individuals, relationships, and systems, not their sacrifice.

If you've been a pastor in a conflicted church, you might identify with the early church martyrs. A second-century account of the martyrs of Lyon—forty-seven Christians who were tortured and killed for their faith—tells how one of them, Blandina, exhausted even her torturers with her endurance under persecution. Kris Culp recounts the story in her book *Vulnerability and Glory: A Theological Account*: "The young slave woman received and bore the glory of God in an exemplary manner. . . . [Her] endurance attested to God's transcendent power over against the empire's prosecution of death" (p. 18). The church goes best when the limits of endurance clarify our faith.

While sacrifice has been a central motif in the Christian tradition, and pastors have long served as the sacrificial lamb, liberation theologies have emerged in the last half-century that recast sacrifice as a means and not an end. Fruitfulness brings restoration, which is the goal—wholeness and a right relationship with God. This is the lesson that the second-century theologian Irenaeus also found in the testimonies of Blandina and the other martyrs. Culp explains, "For Irenaeus it is restoration, not sacrifice—the renewal and repair of the world over against destruction—that epitomized divine power and glory" (p. 20).

Weeding and Pruning, Restore and Renew

Restoration. Renewal. Repair. Righteousness.

The painful conflict that ended my ministry also served as a pruning for me. The church may have thought it was getting rid of a weed, but in truth, the process helped me grow into my spiritual disciplines in a new way. I returned with commitment to what had been a sporadic practice: yoga; the most helpful was the restorative yoga class. One morning, going through the poses, releasing my body and my spirit,

I began to cry. I sank down into the "child's pose," almost a fetal position, curled up, knees under my body, with my head tucked in and down. The instructor, Caren, came over, like a pastor who takes the bread and the cup to someone who cannot find the strength to come forward and receive; she pushed gently on my back, deepening my stretch and encouraging my body to heal. The press of her body against mine was merciful, sacramental. I thought of my friend who had come home after she preached at the funeral of a nine-year-old and melted into her husband's arms. She said, "I could have stayed there all day."

Restoration.

In ReStore, a Habitat for Humanity store where people bring used building materials, proceeds from the sale of shingles and shutters build houses for God's people in need. Whether restoring native prairie grass or wounded souls, leaders are called to weed and prune so human beings and human communities can fulfill their purpose: to receive and to bear the glory of God. It is difficult work. Few people rank it high on their list of chores.

Weeding and Pruning Take Critical Judgment

Clergy prefer the task of support to the task of supervision. Choosing the plants, getting them in the ground, picking the ripe tomatoes off the vine, these are joys. Weeding and pruning? Not so much. It means using critical judgment to end programs that are no longer fruitful but that are still sentimental to some church members. It means offering careful, consistent feedback to staff, particularly in areas in which performance lags. It may mean prioritizing which ministries are most important to the mission of the church rather than to some members of the congregation. It may mean deciding what gets funded first when there are so many needs and not enough resources. It may mean choosing only one person when two are well qualified.

The decisions brought about through weeding and pruning give evidence that transformation has happened. Alex Holsinger—our lead musician and a criminal justice professor, whose particular focus is on prisons and, more specifically, on rehabilitation programs—spoke at a "peace talk" at our young church. Alex spoke about the return rate to prison: over 50 percent. There are too many former prisoners and too few programs aimed at equipping them with skills for the outside world. Alex noted that it is almost worse for those who are received into a program, for the programs are not designed to work, to rehabilitate the person, to help them flourish by giving them the skills to make critical decisions. The programs have design flaws, intentional or not, that actually increase the recidivism rate. It is akin to providing years of guitar lessons but not teaching a person how to place her fingers on the strings and then acting surprised when she cannot play.

Weeding and pruning are critical in order to assess ourselves honestly and to evaluate our poorly calculated decisions and defensive postures. Scott McClellan was among the leaders who packaged the Iraq War, promoted it, and sold it to the American people. When it was evident that the war was going badly, the former White House Press Secretary wrote a best-selling book detailing the hype, deception, and, in some cases, outright lies that were behind the buildup to the war. McClellan is far from alone. I recall an interview with a war correspondent from the *New York Times* who covered the war on terror—from Afghanistan to Abu Ghraib to Guantanamo to Iraq. He was asked, "What happened? How did it come to this?" He explained that after September 11, reporters known for their sharp and critical analysis lost their voice. If reporters raised objections, or questioned a policy, the president merely had to mention anthrax, WMDs, or Al Qaeda and they would shut up.

It's true of all of us. We are too easily shut up, shut down, shut out. That is what I disliked so strongly in McClellan's leadership: his misuse of power and the way he surrendered his responsibility. I see myself in that: stepping aside when I should be stepping up.

Recall the story of Jacob meeting his uncle Laban in Genesis 29. Remember how Jacob wrestled with his brother, Esau, in the womb? Before they are even born, they are competing and fighting. Jacob grabs his brother's heel, hence his name Jacob/yacov: heel, supplanter, over-reacher, trickster. Esau still beats him out of the birth canal, but Jacob is not ready to cede defeat. There is the exchange of food for Esau's birthright when Esau is famished; then there is an alliance with his mother, Rebekah, at the end of his father's life to secure the blessing.

Young Jacob leads in a self-serving, egotistical style. While everyone can see it (thanks to the narrator), Jacob is oblivious to his own flawed leadership style. His power comes at the expense of others. When Rebekah sends her beloved Jacob to her brother Laban's home to find a wife, the rabbis say that it is not just a wife Jacob needs; he needs a mirror, a chance to see in Laban what he was in danger of becoming. The narrator stresses the parallels in their character: Laban greets him with, "You are bone of my bone, flesh of my flesh." But then he treats Jacob like a hired hand, and Jacob finds the shoe, or the sandal, on the other foot when he is in need and Laban does the tricking.

Jacob falls hard for Rachel, Laban's younger daughter, and offers to work seven years for her hand in marriage. Laban says, "It's a deal," but at the end of seven years, in the dark of night, Laban sends his older daughter, Leah, veiled into Jacob's tent. "Why have you deceived me?" Jacob asks, using the same words his father, Isaac, used when Jacob deceived him on his deathbed. Laban's response is a dig at Jacob, "It is not done in our country, to give the younger before the oldest."

It is not just deceit; there is a failure we often see in flawed leadership: the failure to take responsibility. Laban says, "Work another seven years and *we* will give you Rachel, too." As the rabbis say, "We? Who is this 'we'?" Laban acted alone in deceiving Jacob. Leaders step up and use the pronoun "I." There is no "we"—that is, putting our decisions off on others. "I'm responsible. It was my call." Taking responsibility is more than an act of integrity; it is the path to growth.

Weeding and Pruning Take Boldness

When I stepped out of my role, surrendering supervisory responsibilities and ceding too much power to subordinates, I allowed a situation to take root that destroyed the church. Senator Robert Byrd, at one time the longest-serving senator, stood above all others in his passionate, fiery objections to the Iraq War, citing the enormous uncalculated cost in resources and, more, human life. His main objection, though, was granting the president the power to go to war. It was an unprecedented ceding of congressional power. Congress was not totally with the president, but not enough to halt the invasion. I want to lead like Robert Byrd, boldly, fearlessly.

> **Leadership also needs to be weeded and pruned.**

We all need the word of correction, consistent and constructive feedback, someone to prune our branches back and help us grow in new ways. No one benefits when we are too afraid of conflict to share honestly. I took piano lessons for eight years from Mrs. B. She was kind, generous, and patient, and she allowed me to play for eight years without pointing out I wasn't keeping time correctly. I just played and played. When she retired, she sent me to another teacher.

Far more exacting, the new teacher listened to me play for thirty seconds, scowled, and pulled out a beginning piano book. I was discouraged. The longer an incorrect practice has been established, the more difficult it is to change it. Leaders need high expectations and straightforward evaluations. They need to develop and abide by processes that evaluate the mission of the entire organization, particularly their own role as the leader charged with casting a vision.

We may avoid the evaluative process because it requires bold introspection and honesty about our weaknesses, mistakes, brokenness, and, if we are honest, our own potential for annihilation. As the wisdom of old reminds, "Never act as if evil is something that resides solely apart from you." Aware of our capacity for destruction and more significantly attuned to the grace of God, leaders open themselves to feedback and correction for the sake of restoration.

Weeding and Pruning Attend to Competing Values

I have attended to my personal growth, therapeutically and spiritually, since seminary days. The new practices I have developed have come, largely, through the shaping of colleagues and mentors. When it comes to setting a vision, few things can match an exercise in values clarification. Building from Tony Robbins's book *Awaken the Giant Within*, my consultant Dennis Sweeny reminded me that "anytime you are struggling with a decision it is because you have a values conflict. As soon as you get your values understood, your decision will be obvious" (*Awaken the Giant Within: How to*

Take Immediate Control of Your Mental, Emotional, Physical and Financial Destiny [New York: Simon & Schuster, 1992]).

Pruning forces us to consider the shape and direction of present growth and provides an opportunity for stating and ranking often-competing values. Then we can gather the resources necessary to nurture our values.

Weeding and Pruning Require Compassion and Humility

Lidia was annoyed. She, an American Jew from the east coast, was in her early forties. She'd moved to Israel twenty years ago, claimed her citizenship, and never went back home. She was an activist and organizer with an agency trying to resolve the more than sixty-year conflict between the Israelis and the Palestinians. Her office had the familiar look of a not-for-profit organization: worn furniture and a chaotic and harried vibe. The big room was cut into awkward-sized cubicles. Boxes were stacked high. Posters were tacked on every wall, advertising speakers and rallies; others, handwritten, reminded staff to pick up their dishes. They didn't have a space big enough for our group so they circled some chairs in a small cubicle.

They weren't expecting us. We'd arrived at the wrong time or the wrong day. Lidia had been pulled off of another project to offer an overview of their work. That was part of her annoyance, but only part of it. The bigger part was that she'd seen us before—or dozens of groups like ours, that is, American groups. You can always spot us. We are the ones who proudly boast that there are no weeds in our garden. So we trot around the globe, tending to someone else's field. Our group was no different. It was day nine of our trip, and we couldn't understand why they hadn't solved the problems yet. For starters, why hadn't they told the world what was going on there? How the old market in Hebron was now a ghost town because shopkeepers were driven out by settlers?

She listened patiently, and then she responded, "It is out there. There are websites that follow the construction of the separation wall, that track housing demolitions in areas slated for new settlements, that monitor terrorist networks and human rights violations. Maps mark the exact neighborhoods where land has been confiscated, homes bulldozed, olive trees uprooted." We would just rather shop or eat than look at the weeds in our garden. Our country is intolerant of international review, just like I can be defensive when reviewed. Whether those weeds are the inner city, the West Bank, or our own lives, when we name the weeds as weeds, we have to consider changing. Even if practices have not served us or our organizations, it is frightening to leave familiar ground for the unfamiliar.

I almost cried. It was not the annoyance on Lidia's face, but the pained look on her colleague's face. After giving us an overview of their agency's work, Lidia was replaced by Mohammed. He was a dark-skinned Palestinian, thin and soft-spoken. He was bright, no doubt. English was not his first language, though, maybe his third or fourth. At some point a member of our group asked if Lidia could come back

Leaders Weed and Prune

and answer questions. He looked taken aback: "I can answer your questions." I chimed in, "Your sharing is so helpful, but we've heard from very few Israelis. If we could hear a bit more from Lidia?"

He got up and left the cubicle. We could see him talking to Lidia across the way, glancing back and forth at us. Finally they both returned. Mohammed sat back down in the chair, and Lidia, standing above him, said, "I understand your request, but in our office, Israeli and Palestinian speak with one voice. Our work is *joint* work. Separation is the *one* thing we reject. Separation says, 'You are not like us. We will put you on a plantation, behind a wall or a fence, in a ghetto, in a camp.' Resisting separation is central to our work. We name it whenever we see it for the lie that it is."

We understood. But that didn't stop us. Without any humility, for the next half-hour, we asked questions. Now and then we tossed one to Mohammed, but mainly we addressed Lidia. We wanted to hear from an Israeli, a Jew. But, honestly, Lidia was also familiar, Western, American, one of us. I noticed Mohammed's posture, how it changed over the half-hour. The one who was soft spoken but confident was now invisible, unnoticed, unnecessary. Our lack of compassion did that. We had relegated him to the sidelines but also diminished Lidia, their relationship, and what was really important to them. In our rush to understand, we had failed at just that. We had managed to separate them, given Lidia the stage, the power, the microphone. We stripped Mohammed of his voice and his place—divided the world into the guys with the black hats and the guys with the white, the bad seeds and the good.

The great irony of any plant is that you have to prune, sever parts of it, for the plant to thrive over the long run. When Peace Christian Church started, there were those who wanted things to be exactly as they were at Saint Andrew, the structure of the service, every element of worship, down to the benediction. It is pruning that gives a tree its proper form, provides a sound structure, and promotes long life. Given the chance to take their proper form, and have room to grow, we discovered talents in our members that we either never knew about or failed to appreciate. Who knew we had a choir director sitting in the "pews" whose expertise and enthusiasm were literally unrivaled in the city? And two folks who played the saxophone, another who could make the harmonica sing, and enough budding guitarists to fill several garage bands?

Weeding and pruning only work when we work together toward the common good with humility and compassion, when we speak with one voice. This world is one world, loved and held and cherished by one God, the Creator, Redeemer, Healer of all, who sent us One to show us true humility and compassion. Tall Poppy leaders follow our creator God and cultivate these fruits.

chapter six
Leaders Catch the Wind of the Spirit

I read it in my first semester of seminary, and it has guided me ever since—a refrain found in Walter Brueggemann's book *The Prophetic Imagination*: to be a prophet is to be completely with and utterly free from your people (Fortress Press, 1978). That's it. That's what it means to be a pastor, what it means to be a Tall Poppy leader: completely *with* and utterly *free* from the people you serve and lead.

It jumped off of the page because of the tension, the dissonance, the paradox, and the truth of it—*completely with and utterly free from*. That's anything but easy. If you are a pastor or leader of any kind, you know the truth of those words: to be completely with the other—to listen to the angst of your wise, but tender, fourteen-year-old son, not taking your eyes off him, biting your tongue if that is what it takes to keep from stepping in with advice. It's the same challenge when listening to a parishioner or a staff member who is struggling deeply: to be completely with but also utterly free from. To be intensely present, but to hold your own boundaries, your own sense of self, your own moral compass and guide.

To listen, openly, to the ideas and input around you, but then, when the decision time comes, to follow what you know is best and true. To preach from a deep place of God's spirit, confident that preaching the word is what you are called to do, even when it is a difficult and challenging word. *Utterly free from.* It's that *completely with* that allows people to feel God's spirit in your presence, your words, your actions. It's that *free from* that allows you to lead and preach from a place of vision, guided by the Spirit, not popularity or power. I only know how to live and to preach in the Spirit. Every week I try to give it all I've got.

When I was newly married, my husband, who was a chaplain, the pastoral-care type, would say, "I can't believe you said that in the sermon. I can't believe you talked about *that.*" Even if I want to stay away from difficult issues, hide behind a manuscript, use doctrine or dogma to skirt around a topic, I can't seem to. The Spirit is so deep, I preach from the heart and the gut. I read, study, run, pray, and settle on the place where the Scriptures hit me at the deepest point, where it leaves me raw and reeling and hopeful and open to grow.

Most weeks I think that's the right approach because as folks leave, they say, "It feels like you were talking right to me." Of course I wasn't; I was talking to myself. But the human condition is the human condition. When I speak to the deep, desert part of Holly with a word from the well of grace, the chances are that I'll speak to most everyone. But sometimes, when there are painful responses to the word, someone misunderstands an illustration, it hits close to home, or someone doesn't want to be pushed. Then the feeling that all preachers know comes to a deep place, so tender it is almost a physical suffering. And then I think, why do I put myself out there? Why do I risk being vulnerable? I should try the "stained-glass voice" approach to preaching: be boring, dry, distant—and protected.

The longing to be safe and invulnerable and the fear of being rejected and attacked create cautious leaders who learn not to trust the Spirit, who hold back from giving everything they have. All of us know why: we have given our best at times only to be cut down. We can also hold back from giving it all because we want to have something for tomorrow. Any pastor who is worth her salt is encouraged to write a book by her mom and her church members. I heard that for years. Then one day I had a lightning bolt hit me on my run (actually, it was an owl), and I decided to write a book. I got started on it, fast and furious, in usual Holly McKissick style. I went through everything I've preached and picked out the "best of" and put it in four huge binders. I spent the next three months honing a direction, organizing, editing, and crafting a book (which is now in a big binder in my closet under my cowgirl boots).

Then I was asked to write a Lenten devotional book. I needed forty-eight devotionals, and I had all of two months to do it. I'd have to draw from work I'd spent years developing. I was humbled and delighted to be asked, but I also thought there was no way I was going to take my book (which had my "best stuff") and chop it up. So I went to the second-tier reflections on scriptures that were "pretty good."

Halfway through the project, I thought, "This was a mistake. This is not very good." By the end, I thought, "This was just plain dumb." This is the one chance to publish, to leave something behind for my kids, something that will endure, and I've not given my best. A few weeks after I sent the manuscript off, I read Annie Dillard's book *Give It All, Give It Now*. I didn't have much time for reading, because I was trying to catch up on other projects, like my teenagers. But Dillard has distilled her powerful, poetic thoughts down to 121 *words*, a "picture book" for adults. The book is some twenty pages long, with a few words on each page. Three people had given me a copy as a gift. I had given away two; my copy still had the plastic wrap on it. I was curious, too, about the subtitle, *One of the Few Things I Know about Writing*:

> Do not hoard what seems good for a later place in the book, or for another book; give it, give it all, give it now. The impulse to save something good for a better place later is the signal to spend it now. ([New York: Welcome Books, 2009], pp. 1-13)

What if that's true?

"Anything you do not give freely and abundantly becomes lost to you." "These things fill from behind, from beneath like well water." As you give food, the earth makes more; as you give away your money, more comes; as you sing, more songs come; as you give your life, more life comes. These things can happen if we are free, free to catch the Spirit. Leaders catch the wind of the Spirit; they sway free in the breeze. Leaders inspire others to live spirited, passionate, faithful lives.

After David Everson got Johnny Wilson—a young man who was mentally handicapped and spent eleven years in prison for a crime he did not commit—out of prison, David worked on the Innocence Project in Kansas City. He turned his wisdom and commitment from Johnny to the tens of thousands who wither, locked up, for crimes they did not commit. When he was honored with the Charles Evans Whittaker Award, David used his remarks as an invitation to the audience to catch the wind of the Spirit: "I want to use what time I have—what time I have left—to try and get you involved with the Innocence Project."

He told Johnny's story eloquently and powerfully, and he spoke of the outright lies and incompetence that put him in prison. He underlined the team and resources that must be built: Johnny's case alone required twenty people and $1 million. By the end of the speech, there wasn't a dry eye. Then David appealed to the attorneys and the crowd and said something like this: "I am asking you to get involved, to take on cases." He introduced the new director of the Innocence Project and asked the attorneys to give him a card, to volunteer, to help: "I hope to get some of you interested in this work: getting people, innocent people, out of prison, who are actually innocent, serving time for crimes that others committed. Some are serving life sentences; some are on death row. It's not for money, because there isn't any. It's not for fame that fades quickly. Nope. You get the chance to work with other fine lawyers who share this passion. When you tell the story of another person at the mercy of a system, you also tell your own story, what's most important to you. When you work for someone else's freedom, you also work for your own freedom. Freedom from the pettiness and cynicism that is a part of every profession; freedom from chasing things that you know down deep don't really matter to you. In it all, you end up feeling truly alive."

What David was inviting the audience to was this: nothing more and nothing less than living freely and giving all that we have. Catch the wind of the Spirit. Let the passion that is deep within us be called out for this purpose—living a life that is meaningful, worth living. It's living a free, spirited life, being open to the rush of God's spirit in you. It is living the Resurrection.

David received a standing ovation. There was a crowd around him, so I squeezed in to congratulate him and give him a card, and then I left. I walked out behind a group of five young lawyers. A woman said brightly, "Sign me up." The guy next to her chimed in: "I'm ready." "I'm in," said another. Then I heard another voice: "Sure, everyone's all fired up today, but wait until next week. Everyone will be too busy, back to making money."

What is that part of us that resists the Spirit, that pushes our passion down, deeper and deeper still, until it dries up and blows away? Why do we settle for a life lived in the barren, dry places, saying, "No way, I don't think so," to an enlivened life, on the edge, where our true calling lies? In part, we don't want to appear foolish, hopeful, naive. Only a fool puts in everything she has. There is too much to risk; the fear of getting cut down and humiliated is too high. David, who was a professor earlier in his career at the University of Georgia, told me once, "Today, very few lawyers even try a case. Some young lawyers will go through their whole life without trying one." When I asked him why, he said, "They are too afraid of losing, too afraid of making a mistake."

Too afraid of being cut down.

Who hasn't been there? I certainly have, but not very often. I don't want the careful, predictable, calculated position to be "my home." The spirit of God keeps drawing me out, luring me forward, calling me toward God's vision, even when I pull back, when I hesitate.

Bob Berkebile is a Tall Poppy. I don't know how he did it. How he still does it. I don't know how he found the strength to rush into the Hyatt Regency the night of the Skybridge collapse in Kansas City. It was a Friday night in July, 1981. Bob Berkebile had just arrived at a dinner party when the hostess rushed them inside to the breaking news on the television. When he arrived at the scene, there was complete chaos. Fire trucks were rushing in, sirens were wailing, and emergency crews were swarming. When the bridge collapsed, giving way with too much weight on it, dozens of people fell to their death. The skywalks crashed on hundreds below who were dancing and listening to the band that had just begun to play. Glass and metal hurtled through the air, colliding with faces and bodies. In the end there were 114 dead and more than 200 injured.

I know how he got inside: he told the first police officer he saw that he was the architect who designed the building. I don't know how he survived, helping with the rescue effort, wondering, as the bodies were recovered from the debris, "Did I kill these people?" I don't know how he survived the next two years: the endless meetings with attorneys, investigators, victims. Although he was exonerated and the engineering firm was deemed to be at fault, it was an intense time of suffering. To drive through the community and to see what survived of the building probably gave him feelings of shock, grief, isolation, and despair.

From the center of the heat, he survived, like Shadrach, Meschach, and Abednego survived in the fiery furnace. He had angels, the support of others, and a team around him. Survival for any firm connected with the collapse was in question. But they came back and thrived, offering fresh new gifts to the community. We have those angels in our lives.

Two days after I was cut down, I went home for my aunt's funeral. I was in a state of shock; that phase lasted at least eight weeks. I had no preparation for the collapse of something I'd spent years building. The bodies piled up. Through the collapse, my friend Heidi stood beside me. My friend Misty blew like the cool breeze her name suggested, meeting me in Tulsa to make a plan. Heidi stood in front of me to block out more attacks. Cheryl sent chocolate in the mail, and flowers too, but more: she reaffirmed, over and over, my value and worth. Liz offered her ear and similar experience. Cindy and Kris tenderly prodded me to depersonalize the story, to see it as the risk of leadership. Carla brought food and more. My family kept pointing to my roots, deep, and to my future, open.

When we get askew, as we do in conflict, we get worried or angry or afraid, or maybe we get worried, angry, and afraid. We are ashamed, guilt-ridden, fragmented, despairing. A Tall Poppy can get mowed down, knocked over, destroyed by the storms that blow in all directions. Or, if still standing, a Tall Poppy can find it all but impossible to stay focused, to keep reaching toward the light.

Berkebile used the next few years for intense reflection: holding a mirror up to his life and his life's work. Taught by the gifted Buckminster Fuller, Berkebile began to wonder about the value of his field. Sure, they had pleased their clients. But what were they doing for the health and well-being of the occupants of their buildings or the vitality of the earth? Berkebile emerged from the collapse to stand tall, resilient. He caught the wind of the Spirit and went on to become a singular leader in green architecture. From projects to legislation, he stands out in the field, putting his spade in first, reaching deeper and deeper to find alternative, responsible ways to create.

I was in the Hyatt Regency for the annual dinner of the Innocence Project. There was a huge crowd. John Grisham was the speaker. Members of my church were on the podium, but my thoughts went to the collapse. Every time I'm in the Hyatt in Kansas City—never mind the name of the hotel is now different—I think of the collapse, perhaps because as a young, impressionable pastor, I met several survivors who were deeply scarred years afterward. There is no plaque marking the space, but longtime Kansas citizens don't need it. This evening, though, I thought of Bob Berkebile. His story could not be further from that of Darryl Burton, my friend and colleague, who spent almost twenty-five years in prison for a murder he didn't commit. Yet, Bob and Darryl want the same thing, the same thing I want: to live free, to hear proclamations of grace, acceptance, innocence.

I need to hear, over and over, that my sins are nothing compared to the grace of God. My lifetime of mistakes means nothing compared to the sweet wonder of God's spirit. It takes a long time for the truth to come out, sometimes years. I listened to another guide, Mary Zimmerman, a professor of women's studies and sociology of medicine. She'd been in the struggle for three decades and then some. I listened while she, a Tall Poppy herself, told me how women, in particular, hold their truth—from the wounds of the bedroom to the boardroom to the battlefield. She was right. It took three months and then some to get the story of the plot against me "out." But, by that point, I realized the real truth was a far greater gift than I'd imagined in the first ten weeks of the struggle.

Freedom. Oh, freedom. Oh, freedom. Oh yes, I know. The "truth" was out about me: not perfect, not even close. There were e-mails, harvested and hoarded and then sent off to destroy my ministry and my name. At first, it was horrifying and humiliating. Then there was a fight, waged to win my honor and the truth. But over time something happened: I came to see the truth in it. Yep, I use salty language. Yes, my passion runs both ways. Yep, I talk too fast for others to follow. I do not always complete my sentences. Sometimes I say harsh things; sometimes I feel, and even act, entitled. No hiding it. There was no way to put it back. Like the saying goes, "You can't put the genie back in the bottle." Yet, that is finally where the hope is found.

It's the story of Pandora's box. Once opened, it all flies out: hatred, anger, envy, the lies, the hurt. You try and put it back in, and what you find, finally, at the very bottom is hope. That's all there is. It's not hope in being vindicated. It's not hope in your purity, your exceptionalism. It's hope born of this truth: you are free. You aren't what others think you are, really. You aren't valued because of what people believe about you or your actions.

My daughter, Eden, called from school and said, "I'm feeling like a Tall Poppy today."

My heart melted.

Unconditional love.

That's what it was.

Unconditional.

What does it mean to look at your child and really know? My love for you has nothing to do with your grade point average, the cleanliness of your room, your PSAT score. My love is unconditional. I want you safe, whole, full of joy and delight.

No one had stopped to help my daughter. Her car spun three times on the interstate; she swerved to keep from hitting the concrete embankment; she overcorrected and went into the ditch on the right shoulder. She came to rest with her car facing the oncoming traffic. Pinned in, she couldn't open the door. Her phone flew to the back seat. She sat there for ten full minutes, trying to calm down and make a plan. In the dark night, she waited till there was a break in the traffic; then she gunned it and flew back around. She is a Tall Poppy, too.

Now things were in perspective and my priorities were straight. I was free to catch the Spirit and leave old wounds behind. My loved ones are what is truly important, and that is why we upped and moved as soon as the call came from Peace Church.

He was a Tall Poppy—creative, caring, brilliant—a beautiful man and an incredible pastor. He moved to Missouri to take a church call about the same time as I did. His new church didn't know that he was gay or that he had AIDS.

After his ministry ended, he volunteered to help me with my new church start. Even at the end, he stood tall, shriveled to ninety pounds, his face covered with lesions and sores. Still, tall: generous, accepting, forgiving.

I don't know anyone who loved church like he did. He never missed worship. He'd pull up in the sports car that his partner bought for him, carrying a vase of peonies for the Communion table bigger than he was. I remember sitting with him the winter before he died. He was in a hospital bed in his living room looking through the back window. He was making a map of where his bulbs were to go, imagining the spring, plotting the resurrection.

He rebounded again and again. Strong and determined, he outlived the doctor's predictions, defied their "best case" scenarios repeatedly: a Tall Poppy. He dropped by my house one day, unannounced, with one more detail about his memorial service. He stressed that what he wanted was to say thank you. To say thank you to everyone—to family, friends, even to the church when it had rejected him. What he said next was nothing short of amazing: "I'm so thankful for AIDS. Without it, I'd never have met my doctor, the nurses, all the people at the free family health clinic. Before I had AIDS, I was never alive."

Thinking of him, E. B. White's richly evocative description of his wife, Katharine, planting bulbs in her dying days, comes to mind. Katharine S. White published only one book—a collection of articles on gardening for the *New*

Yorker. E. B. White crafted the book after she died; a gift he credited with saving his life, bringing her words to him even in her absence. In the foreword, White described this small fragile figure defying age and weather:

> As the years went by and age overtook her, there was something comical yet touching in her bedraggled appearance on this awesome occasion—the small, hunched-over figure, her studied absorption in the implausible notion that there would be yet another spring, oblivious to the ending of her own days, which she knew perfectly well was near at hand, sitting there with her detailed chart under those dark skies in the dying October, calmly plotting the resurrection. (E. B. White, foreword to Katharine S. White's *Onward and Upward in the Garden* [Boston: Beacon Press, 2002])

That is how I want to live and die: calmly plotting the resurrection—for myself, but more, for God's beloved community. A community called to stand tall, to look out, ahead, with expectation of yet more good gifts—inexplicable, gracious, merciful—to come.

Resilience. Resurrection. The gracious life of a Tall Poppy leader.

www.ingramcontent.com/pod-product-compliance
Lightning Source LLC
Chambersburg PA
CBHW011954150426
43198CB00020B/2929